*"Who ran to help me when I fell, And would some pretty story tell, Or kiss the place to make it well? My mother."*

–Jane Taylor (1783–1824)

# *D*edication

Helen Pearce O'Bryant and Jewel Pearce Patterson, 1989

*I Remember Mama* is dedicated to my own beloved and greatly missed Mama, Jewel Estelle Pearce Patterson (1910-2002), for her absolute and unconditional love; her inspiration and insistence that I face all challenges and accept no limitations; the examples she set that I am still trying to live up to; her many long hours of hard work to rear me, educate me, and give me every opportunity; her incredible strength, courage, and compassion in dealing with adversity; her creative spirit that led her to make the most of life; her unswerving belief in those she cared for; and her willingness to help, understand, counsel, and most of all, love…and in memory of all those beautiful dresses she made me!

---

*I Remember Mama* is also dedicated to my *other* mother, Helen Lydia Pearce O'Bryant, Mama's sister. My adored Aunt Helen took over my mothering when I was only three months old, after Mama had been badly hurt in a car accident, and she has been a rock of support for me not only for that first year of my life but forever after. She'd drive 40 miles to bring me soup when I was sick or answer a midnight summons to the hospital when only her gentle touch could get me to sleep. She comforted and chastised, defended and praised; she always included Mama and me in her own loving family; and she taught me the peace of a happy home.

---

How lucky I am to have had these two strong, wise, and loving women in my life— "the mothers," as they were affectionately termed by both family and friends. *I Remember Mama*…both of them!

*"You may have tangible wealth untold; Caskets of [jewels] and coffers of gold. Richer than I you can never be— I had a mother who read to me."*

—Strickland Gillilan

# Introduction

*The I Remember Mama Project was created in loving memory of my mother, Jewel Pearce Patterson (1910-2002). The project has been a joy because so many wonderful quilts have been created in honor and in memory of so many mothers and because it has allowed quilt artists to create work that deals positively with their memories—good and bad—and with the losses of their mothers. It is said that the mother is the first, most important, and most formative relationship in a person's life. I know that is true for me, and after seeing all these special quilts and reading the artists' statements, I believe it must be a universal truth. Each of us has only one mother. How blessed we are to have her, whether she is alive today to love us or whether she lives only in our hearts and minds.*

—Karoline (Karey) Helen Patterson Bresenhan

So many of my memories of Mama are all tied up with quilts.

As a baby, I must confess to having no memories at all of Mama holding me in the baby quilt she made—pink on one side and blue on the other, made when a mother had no way to know the gender of her baby—and yet, even today, that is still the quilt I reach for on chilly nights.

As a little girl, I remember clearly how Mama would tiptoe into my bedroom in the wee hours of the morning when a Texas blue norther had hit, dropping the temperature severely, with an armload of quilts she piled on me...so many I could barely turn over under their weight!

As a teenager, I remember taking her green Double Wedding Ring quilt, part of her trousseau of 12 quilts, to the beach for a picnic and being soundly chastised when I got back home! For years, she swore I had lost that quilt, but long after I married, I found it tucked in the deep, dark recesses of her linen closet.

As a newly engaged graduate student, I remember Mama using a plate and a cup to mark the quilting designs on my very own wedding quilt, right before

all the great-aunts arrived for the family quilting bee where our grandmother taught my cousin and me to quilt.

As a young antiques dealer with too much space and too few antiques, I remember Mama bringing over a carload of family quilts, spreading them out on the almost empty shop floor, and gently suggesting that I hang them to hide the vacant areas...which I did happily.

As director of America's largest quilt event, the International Quilt Festival in Houston, I still remember those beautiful family quilts, which became a hallmark of my shop, later became the basis of our first quilting classes—taught by Mama, of course!—and still later led to the founding of Festival more than 30 years ago. So many people loved them that I created the shows to give them the chance to learn about and acquire good quilts and created the classes to teach them how to make quilts.

As a loving daughter, I remember how Mama never willingly missed a minute of all the Festival excitement, right up until the 2002 show a few weeks before she died. When she didn't come that year, I knew that, sadly, it would soon be my turn to have to say, "I Remember Mama." But oh, what rich memories she left me!

My mama was so strong and so intelligent that she could have been president of General Motors, Harvard University, or of the United States. But Mama was born only 10 years after the end of the 19th century, and those were not her opportunities. Instead, she made it her business to make everyone around her happy and to bring beauty and creativity to as many people as she could manage to reach. What a legacy.

When she fell in love, she fell head over heels. She met my daddy on a blind date and six weeks later, she married him. Her father was so angry that the "apple of his eye" would go off and leave him that he refused even to attend her wedding. Her love affair ended tragically 20 years later

"*Life began with waking up and loving my mother's face.*"
–George Eliot

when my daddy was accidentally shot by what we thought was an unloaded gun. Mama was a beautiful woman when she was widowed at 43, but she was never tempted by another man. She had had her one great love.

Mama believed to her core in education. She was valedictorian of her junior college, and when she was widowed, she promptly went back to college, while working full-time and sewing for "her ladies" most nights… because she had to get that four year degree that would allow her to support us and educate me. Later, she got her Master of Library Science degree.

Mama loved to create— dresses, quilts, surprises. She could create a formal gown that made even a "less-endowed" teenager feel glamorous and orchestrate anything and make it wonderful. One of my favorite Christmases was the old-fashioned one at Granny's that Mama and Aunt Helen masterminded. We kids were stunned at the 12-foot tree decorated with cookies, apples and oranges, and ropes of cranberries and popcorn…a tree like our mothers remembered.

Mama was probably the most determined person I have ever known. I came down with polio in the epidemic of 1948. Mama nursed me herself. The standard treatment then was hot packs. Mama set up a hot plate in a west bedroom, cut up an old blue wool bathrobe, boiled those wool strips, fished them out of the boiling water with a broomstick, and wrung them out with her bare hands before wrapping my leg in them. I cried, I blistered, I begged her not to keep on—but hour after hour, there came those smelly blue wool hot packs. Even after her own hands had blistered badly, she kept on wringing them out and wrapping me up. I came through with only mild paralysis, solely because of Mama. To this day, I would define misery as the smell of boiled wool on a hot August afternoon.

Because our mothers were sisters and very close, my cousins Nancy and Hollis and I were blessed with two mothers. Nancy remembers that motherhood was shared equally between our mothers, and we three children reported to whichever Mother was on duty. Aunt Helen was the dreamer, but Mama was the doer, who

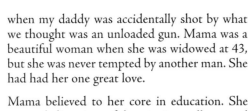

always knew how to tackle a project, whether it was painting elaborate Christmas cookies for all the children in our three classes, leaving carrot tops all over the sidewalk to keep me believing in the Easter Bunny, or mailing Nancy home-grown camellias when she was away at college.

Mama was a fourth generation Texas quilter who taught quilting in Houston and other cities, but who taught mostly at my former quilt shop, Great Expectations Quilts. She had a devoted following of students who adored her. She was not only their quilting teacher, she was also their friend, their mentor, their advisor. She dispensed advice on work, cooking, sewing, young husbands, health, children, jobs, older husbands, babies, and aging parents (never thinking of herself that way, of course!) just as easily as she recommended colors and fabrics. Mama almost never met a stranger, for it was the rare stranger who did not become her friend. She made many beautiful quilts in her life, but her most important legacy—other than her family—was the love of quilts that she instilled in so many people over the two decades that she taught quilting.

I had Mama longer than most people have their mothers, and I treasure those years—the good times we had, the gorgeous clothes she made, the advice she dispensed, the interest she showed, the help she gave…but most especially, I treasure the absolute and unconditional love she gave me. As Nancy said, "she was truly a force of nature, like the moon, the stars, the tide. To think that she is gone is to think the tide will never come in, the moon will cease shining, the stars will go out. And so we know that she is not gone, but only changed, and that her love, like ours, goes on. And we are comforted by that thought."

Mama was my one constant in a world of change, and oh, how I miss her. She truly was the wind beneath my wings.

*"A mother is she who can take the place of all others but whose place no one else can take."*

—Cardinal Mermillod

# about the Project

*The Home Place*, Bernadette Pohl

When my mother, Jewel Estelle Pearce Patterson, died on her 92nd birthday in 2002, I wanted to do something special to honor her memory, and nothing seemed more appropriate for someone who had taught thousands of people to love quilts, and to love to make quilts, than a quilt exhibit and competition. That's how the three-year *I Remember Mama* project came to be.

The first phase of the project began in 2003 and resulted in one of the most popular exhibits ever presented at the International Quilt Festival in Houston—*I Remember Mama: The Hand That Rocked the Cradle*. The 50,000+ visitors to the show laughed, cried, and reminisced as they worked their way through the 67 quilts in the invitational exhibit. In 2003, the second phase of the project—*I Remember Mama: My Mother, My Family, and Me*—was shown, again to great acclaim. These 36 quilts were the products of family teams; some were original quilts, while others were generational pieces that began with an inherited quilt top or quilt pieces and were finished for the exhibition.

In the third and final phase of the project—*I Remember Mama*—quilts were entered in an international competition, and 61 quilts were selected to be seen at the International Quilt Festival in 2005. Exciting prizes were awarded by the judge, Mary Leman Austin, executive director of *Quilter's Newsletter Magazine*. The Grand Prize—$5000 cash and a trip for two to Europe to see *I Remember Mama* on exhibit at Patchwork and Quilt Expo in Lyon, France—was won by Pat Moormann Kumicich for *Rosemarie—Now and Then*. The second prize, $2500 cash, went to Carol Suto for *Monday Morning 1955*. Third place of $1000 was awarded to Mary Beth Clark for *The Last Squeeze*. Five honorable mentions of $200 each were awarded to: Geeg Aaker for *Pleiades Ladies*; Karen Hanken for *Nana—Our Lady of Glenside*; Lyric Montgomery Kinard for *The Women of God Know This*; Ruth Powers for *Bittersweet Memories*; and Marlene Brown Woodfield for *In My Mother's Arms*.

Following its premiere in Houston, *I Remember Mama* is touring internationally, with venues such as the International Quilt Festival in Chicago in April, 2006; Patchwork and Quilt Expo in Lyon, France in June, 2006; and several museums, including the New England Quilt Museum in 2007.

The *I Remember Mama* project invited quilters to create quilts depicting the memories, joys, dreams, thoughts, ideals, challenges, frustrations, and sorrows of motherhood. This book collects all 164 of the quilts from the three years in full color photographs and includes the moving and evocative artist's statements as well. Together, the exhibit and the book present a powerful tribute to the joys and pains of generations of grandmothers, mothers, and "other" mothers—aunts, foster mothers, mothers-in-law, and mother figures. *I Remember Mama* was created out of love for one mother—my own—but it culminated in a project of love for many mothers.

As President Abraham Lincoln once said, "*All that I am I owe to my angel mother.*" How true!

—KAROLINE (KAREY) HELEN PATTERSON BRESENHAN

"*Motherhood: All love begins and ends there.*"
—ROBERT BROWNING

# table of ontents

*is for the* **million** *things she gave me,*

*means* **only** *that she's growing old,*

*is for the* **tears** *she shed to save me,*

*is for her* **heart** *of purest gold;*

*is for her* **eyes,** *with love-light shining,*

*means* **right,** *and* **right** *she'll always be,*

Put them all together, they spell

*'mother'*

A word that means the world to me.

—HOWARD JOHNSON

2005

I REMEMBER Mama

Within the quilt image:

I remember Mama liked to fish, play bingo and poker.
She worked hard but still found time to volunteer
at the hospital. She loves peanuts and chocolate.
I remember the day she went into the nursing home.
Yes, I remember Mama —
I wish Mama could remember me.

## ROSEMARIE—NOW AND THEN
**Pat Moormann Kumicich**
*Naples, Florida*
*37" x 52"*

**Materials:** *Cotton, cheesecloth, UltraSuede®*
**Techniques:** *Machine appliqué and piecing, free-motion machine embroidery and quilting, printing on fabric, painting*

## GRAND PRIZE WINNER

My mother, Rosemarie Bernier Moormann (1919-2005), suffered from dementia for many years. She enjoyed watching me sew, and in her earlier, healthier times she was very supportive of my art. She died one month to the day after I finished this quilt. I'm grateful that I was with her for her last breath. I'm quite certain that, for a second, she knew who I was and offered me a last kiss.

## MONDAY MORNING 1955
**Carol Suto**
*San Leandro, California*
49" x 38"

**Materials:** *Cotton, some hand-painted, fabric from old clothing*
**Techniques:** *Painted background, appliqué and fused figures, machine quilting*

## 2ND PLACE WINNER

On Monday mornings, with sunny skies and brisk winds, my mother—Caroline "Carrie" Lardo Duhan (1915-2002)—hung her wash on the backyard clothesline. I loved to "help" by hanging hankies and running through the clothes that were flying on the lines. I can still remember the sound, the smell, and the feel of the wet sheets slapping at my face.

"There is only one *pretty child* in the world, and *every mother* has it."

—CHINESE PROVERB

## THE LAST SQUEEZE
### Mary Beth Clark
*South Elgin, Illinois*
62" x 37"

**Materials:** *Cotton, taffeta*
**Techniques:** *Raw edge piecing, zigzag stitching,
machine quilting*

## 3RD PLACE WINNER

I was eight years old when my mother, Betty Wolff Bierley (1921-1959), died unexpectedly. The last precious memory I have of her is sharing a tight hug. I wanted to capture that hug in a quilt design and layer into fabric some of the confusing feelings of loss and pain. The grief has faded, but the memory of that squeeze has lasted my lifetime. (*Second in a series*)

"A mother is a person who *seeing there are* only four pieces of pie for five people, *promptly announces* she never did care for pie."

—TENNEVA JORDAN

### PLEIADES LADIES
**Geeg Aaker**
*Elko, Minnesota*
*71" x 80"*

**Materials:** *Cotton, some hand-dyed or photocopied, fabric markers*
**Techniques:** *Fused appliqué, machine piecing and quilting, faces and arms painted with fabric dyes*

## HONORABLE MENTION

Six of the Seven (Quilting) Sisters are my "Heavenly Mothers" (left to right): Arleen Langhoff Aaker (1911-1998), my mother-in-law; Lizzie Keithahn Kiester (1888-1969), my maternal grandmother; Lina Seegers Kiester (1859-1932), my maternal great-grandmother; Marie Garbers Keithahn (1847-1931), my maternal great-grandmother; Monetta Goetz Schendel (1893-1977), my paternal grandmother; and Kaye Kiester Schendel (1916-1981), my mother.

All of them were "handy with a needle." They were midwives with me as I labored with this quilt. They comforted me with memories: the curve of my mother's mouth, the arthritic hands of my mother-in-law, the manicured fingers of one grandmother, and the work-etched hands of my other grandmother. They encouraged me with cherished gifts of their handmade quilts, childhood birthday-boxes of sewing notions, and a creative spirit. As I sit at the lower end of the table, I hardly feel worthy to join them in the making of their quilt. Yet I smile to myself, that they have called me to join them to carry on their sewing tradition. I will not let them down. I wear the seventh star with honor.

## THE WOMEN OF GOD KNOW THIS
**Lyric Montgomery Kinard**
*Cary, North Carolina*
48" x 25"

**Materials:** *Hand-dyed cotton, thread*
**Techniques:** *Dyeing, discharging, fusing, machine quilting*

## HONORABLE MENTION

Pictured are (left to right) Ruth May Marble Hoisington (great-grandmother, 1906-1988), Martha Acenath Hakes Marble (great-great-grandmother, 1871-1955), Nancy Lee Montgomery Gillins (aunt, b1942), and Edith Ruth Hoisington Montgomery (grandmother, 1921-1982). When I struggle with the difficult task of motherhood, I look to the ancestors and mothers who have come before me, from whom I have much to learn. This quote by Neil A. Maxwell says what I feel of their work and mine. *"When the real history of mankind is fully disclosed, will it feature the echoes of gunfire or the shaping sound of lullabies? The great armistices made by military men or the peacemaking of women in homes and in neighborhoods? Will what happened in cradles and kitchens prove to be more controlling than what happened in congresses? When the surf of the centuries has made the great pyramids so much sand, the everlasting family will still be standing, because it is a celestial institution, formed outside celestial time. The women of God know this."*

Before you were conceived
I wanted you
Before you were born
*I loved you*
Before you were here   an hour
I would die for you
This is the miracle of life.

- MAUREEN HAWKINS

## BITTERSWEET MEMORIES
### Ruth Powers
*Carbondale, Kansas*
50" x 62"

**Materials:** *Cotton, various cotton, rayon and metallic threads, one crystal teardrop*
**Techniques:** *Machine piecing and quilting*

## HONORABLE MENTION

When they were young, my French-Canadian grandparents immigrated to this country in search of a better life. Times were hard, and he gave her a small rifle, so that she might augment the meager stew-pot. She shot one rabbit with that gun and was so devastated that she sat on a nearby stump and cried. She never used the gun again. Grammy, Rose Cormier Casey (1892-1982), was a very strong, hard working, and compassionate woman who loved all animals.

Many, many years later, my grandfather gave the rifle to me, saying that I should have it because it was a "girl's gun." I learned to shoot with it—targets only, because, like my grandmother, I had no desire to shoot any living thing. My father took the gun from me and gave it to my brother, the favored child. I do not know where the rifle is now, but wherever it is, I know that it is mine, the only thing given to me by my grandparents.

**IN MY MOTHER'S ARMS**
Marlene Brown Woodfield
*La Porte, Indiana*
24" x 48"

**Materials:** *Cottons and blends*
**Techniques:** *Hand and machine appliqué, machine quilting*

# HONORABLE MENTION

Cradled in my mother's arms, I was presented for baptism into the family of God. After my parents' marriage, my father became ill with tuberculosis and went west for eight years of treatment. I was their first born and arrived after nine years of waiting. Later, another daughter and a son were added to complete this loving family of five. This portrait is of Ruth Ludders Brown (1909-1995) and her daughter, Marlene.

## NANA—OUR LADY OF GLENSIDE
**Karen Hanken**
*Jacksonville, Oregon*
*36" x 54"*

**Materials:** *Cotton, cotton and rayon thread*
**Techniques:** *Machine piecing, quilting, and embroidery*

# HONORABLE MENTION

Her home was a refuge to anyone in need; the phone always rang, strangers came to her door. She sheltered the battered, housed the homeless, nursed the disabled, and fed the lonely. Born an American to Italian immigrants, she embodied the spirit of her cherished country and of the Blessed Mother to whom she prayed.

My Grandmother: her name was Millie, but everyone called her Nana. Remembering Carmela Rosa "Millie" Romeo Minio (1908-2003).

## DAUGHTERS OF DAUGHTERS
**Mary Beth Frezon Goodman**
*Brainard, New York*
*43" x 43"*

**Materials:** *Cotton fabric, rayon and cotton threads, glass beads*
**Techniques:** *Machine piecing, appliqué, and quilting, beading*

Thinking of childhood memories created a list of small moments and big lessons. As my list (seen in the quilt's background and printed on a back label) got longer, I wondered about my parents' memories of their parents. Suddenly I was surrounded by generations—daughters who grew up and taught their daughters by example. Sons and daughters, we're all children of children. Remember. Live. Teach. Inspired by my parents: Elizabeth Mulligan Frezon (b1930) and Edward Gerald Frezon (b1932).

## BACKYARD MEDITATION
**Cynthia Morgan**
*Boulder, Colorado*
*24" x 17"*

**Materials:** *Cotton*
**Techniques:** *Raw edge appliqué, machine piecing,*
*free-motion machine quilting*

Mom loved hanging laundry on the clothesline outside in her own backyard. She loved the fresh smell of it, but mostly she loved the chance to be outside, alone in the quiet of the sunny morning, doing something enjoyable yet useful.

She was a divorced mother of four and worked a full-time job to put a roof over our heads and food on the table. On Saturdays, we awoke to sounds of the clunky old washing machine and knew she was out hanging that first load of wash. It was one chore she wouldn't let anyone else do. She went about it slowly, almost leisurely, and in a specific order: sheets on the front line, then towels, shirts and dresses, and finally on the very back line, next to the tall wood fence, the underwear was hung modestly.

I cannot see laundry drying on a clothesline, as rare a thing as it is now, without a deep yearning for my sweet, hard-working mother, Jacqueline Nedrud Morgan (1921-2000).

*"A mother's*
*love endures*
*through all."*

—WASHINGTON IRVING (1783 - 1859)

## THE MANY FACES OF HAZEL
### Tina Abernethy
*Montgomery, Texas*
51" x 51"

**Materials:** *Cotton, fabric photo sheets*
**Techniques:** *Quilted scrapbook look, embellishment*

My mother, Hazel Miller Lohse (1918-2002), wore many hats—a wife and mother who sang at the USO clubs during World War II, a person who loved to bake and sew. When she discovered quilting, a new passion emerged. She lived for the annual International Quilt Festival in Houston and got me addicted as well! Mom developed Alzheimer's in her later years and succumbed to it in 2002. This is a memorial to her.

## GRANDMA MAGGIE
**Peg Keeney**
*Harbor Springs, Michigan*
34" x 40"

**Materials:** *Cotton and silk*
**Techniques:** *Raw edge appliqué, machine quilting, hand embroidery*

My grandmother, Margaret Walcott Webster DesRocher (1885-1978), the most significant person in my life, was fiercely independent, incredibly resourceful, and relished a good challenge. For their first anniversary, Grandpa bought her a treadle sewing machine and five yards of silk. She made herself a tucked leghorn sleeve blouse! Over the years Grandma took in sewing; later she branched out into millinery. In the 1930's, Grandma began to take in boarders, often elderly women. While my three children were growing up, they always referred to her home as the "House of Grandmothers." This quilt was designed from an old sepia photograph of Grandma climbing a fence on a summer day. I hope that it captures her spirit.

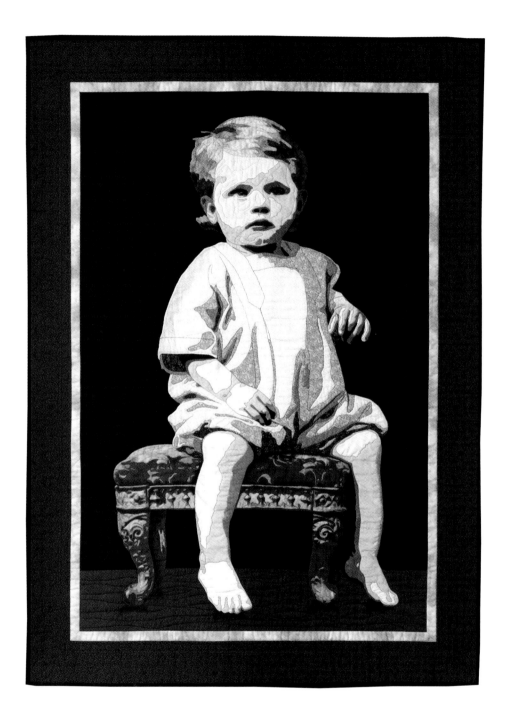

### THE LITTLE ORPHAN
**Bonnie Quick Keller**
*Chehalis, Washington*
*40" x 55"*

**Materials:** *Cotton and hand-dyed fabrics*
**Techniques:** *Photo scanning, computer posterizing, fabric printing, appliqué, machine quilting*

My mother, Laura Ebbesen Quick (1912-2002), was orphaned at birth and was placed in a Danish orphanage in Tyler, Minnesota. The photo used for the quilt was taken sometime around her first birthday. She spoke only Danish until her maiden aunt took her in and raised her from the age of three. Mother was a strong woman who raised five children (I was the middle child). She died at the age of 90.

## MAMA RUTH
**Pamela Allen**
*Kingston, Ontario, Canada*
*40" x 44"*

**Materials:** *Recycled fabrics, remnants*
**Techniques:** *Raw edge appliqué, machine quilting, embellishment*

At the age of nine, because of family turmoil, I was fostered for a year. I was hurt and frightened but had the good fortune to be cared for by a wonderful woman who welcomed me into her boisterous family of three boys. She was loving and demonstrative…she made me stewed rhubarb when no one else liked it! At 40, I succeeded in finding her so I could thank her for her kindness. It was then that I learned I was one of 17 children she had fostered—all girls. This is a tribute to Ruth Oxley—"Mama Ruth," as I called her—who made a big difference in lots of girls' lives.

## THE MOTHER OF GIRL SCOUTS
**Jamie Fingal**
*Orange, California*
21" x 32"

**Materials:** *Batik fabrics, fabric marker*
**Techniques:** *Fused appliqué, photo transfer, machine quilting*

This quilt honors my hero and mentor, Juliette Gordon Low (1860-1927), who, when she was over 50 and almost deaf, started the Girl Scouts in Savannah, Georgia in 1912. The fact that she never let her deafness, back problems, or cancer keep her from full participation in life encourages me to push past any challenges I may encounter and keep my eyes on my dreams. Juliette's dream lives on as Girl Scouts continues as the pre-eminent organization for girls in the U.S.A.

## HER FUTURE WAS BRIGHT
**Frances Holliday Alford**
*Austin, Texas*
44" x 60"

**Materials:** *Dupioni silk, scanned pages, tulle*
**Techniques:** *Painting on organza, photo transfers, embellishment overlaid with tulle, machine quilting*

A snapshot from my parents' wedding inspired this piece, which honors my mother, Nancy Hayes Holliday (1915-1971). She looked so happy and so hopeful. I used images from my own early childhood imposed on a crocheted apron. One apron string is woven into her bridal bouquet. The entries in the baby book and the letter from her father show that she had looked forward to motherhood with great joy. Because my mother believed that educated mothers produce educated offspring, I have included images of both our diplomas. My mother had six children in 13 years, lived life fully, and died at 55. She left way too soon. We miss her.

## A JOURNEY OF LOVE
**Janet Grey**
*Taupo, New Zealand*
*38" x 67"*

**Materials:** *Cotton, vintage velvet, satin*
**Techniques:** *Appliqué, hand quilting, fabric painting, fabric weaving*

These childhood scribble patterns seemed an appropriate way of putting memories into fabric. The design begins at the bottom with Nana—my maternal grandmother, Bessie Denniston Landels (1883-1967)—taking me on a journey of learning and love. She taught me skills—weaving baskets, sewing, preserving, and gardening—and instilled a love of family, fabric, creating, and nature. She left heaps of memories such as podding (shelling) peas and beans together, always having to wear pinnies (aprons), making hundreds of dolls, playing croquet and card games, and button jars. She told me stories of a pioneer childhood in the late 1800's on a farm with massive rabbit problems. I adored my Nana.

## MY DEAR SAINTED MOTHER AND HER ONE-EYED DOG
**Mary Ethel McBride**
*DeLand, Florida*
*23" x 36"*

**Materials:** *Cottons, silk dress made by mother, dog's Picasso eye and fur from friends*
**Techniques:** *Mostly hand stitching, beading, fusing*

I gave my mother a puppy because she wouldn't exercise her knee replacement and she was lonely. Ethel and Foofer (born Fool for Love on April 1) had a terrible beginning because he refused to be potty trained. She was going to give him back, but when he ran into the car door and lost his eye, she felt that God was punishing her, as she could not return him damaged. Foofer learned to potty outdoors, and they became one in their love and loyalty to each other. After 12 years, her little dog died on his 13th birthday, and my mother, Mary Ethel Robinson Fincke (1920-2004), died 22 days later.

## PATTIE'S SAMPLER
**Mary Ann Herndon**
*Spring, Texas*
*46" x 59"*

**Materials:** *Hand-dyed fabrics, Perle cotton thread*
**Techniques:** *Machine piecing and quilting, fused appliqué*

When I began this tribute to my mother, Bonnie Rae Hale Jackson (1911-1995), my children and I started remembering all the traits that made her the person she was. Thus, the ABC's of my mother took form.

My mother did much of the parenting alone since my father was a naval engineer at sea for long periods. When she died, I found records of all sorts and scrapbooks containing every honor her children had achieved. But the detailed accounts of her grocery purchases that she kept to show my father were the most reveal-ing—my mother was accountable and could justify everything she did. Mother was a unique and loving person who unselfishly put everyone before herself. She was truly an extraordinary mom.

## TIANA
**Gayla McAlary**
*San Diego, California*
*60" x 80"*

**Materials:** *Cotton*
**Techniques:** *Machine piecing, hand appliqué, hand quilting*

My mother is Native American Indian, a member of the Wyandotte Nation, raised in Oklahoma. As a young girl she dreamed of being a ballet dancer. Life happened, and at 14 she married and then had five children, putting her dream to rest. She always taught me and my siblings that we could do or be anything that we wanted. I am now one of a handful of female yacht captains sailing around the world and making a few quilts along the way.

When I read about this contest I started *Tiana*, and when my mother saw my work, it inspired her to take her first ballet lesson at the age of 61.

## HOLDING BOTH ENDS FROM THE MIDDLE
### Mary Beth Bellah
*Charlottesville, Virginia*
*28" x 72"*

**Materials:** *Cotton and sheer fabric, copper mesh*
**Techniques:** *Layering, machine and hand quilting, embellishment*

Only now, as my daughter, 18, stands on the threshold of her own adult journey, can I begin to comprehend the emotions behind that rueful, proud, loving look that would come over my mother's face each time I headed back out to college, out to my first home, out to my own family. I've just realized I'm in the middle, holding onto both of these special women in my life: my mother, Elizabeth "Buff" Bixby Voelker (b1940) and my daughter, Jessica Rae Bellah (b1986).

## LOSING HYACINTH
### Pat Doyle Mikrut
*Palos Park, Illinois*
*22" x 22"*

**Materials:** *Cotton, some hand-dyed, tulle,*
*rayon and metallic threads*
**Techniques:** *Thread painting, free-motion embroidery*

She nurtured a family, built a library, sewed my wedding gown, and cuddled her grandchildren. But then she forgot how to sew, bake, knit, and garden. She couldn't find her way home. When words got lost, she stopped speaking. She didn't know her husband, children, grandchildren, or friends. She was gone long before she died. I wish I could recall what she was like before the Alzheimer's, when she was still Hyacinth. This quilt is about my mother, Hyacinth Eileen Kierig Doyle (1915-1987).

## MAMA'S BLUE PERIOD
### Betsy True
*Alexandria, Virginia*
*27" x 38"*

**Materials:** *Cotton, batik, photo transfer fabric, bead*
**Techniques:** *Photo transfer, machine appliqué and quilting*

Going through family heirlooms, I discovered photos of my mother— Mary Jane Pasalich Hamas (1925-2002). They showed her at home in Hibbing, Minnesota; dating my father; newly married; and as a new mother. It was like meeting her for the first time. I decided to make a quilt using those pictures that would reflect her life as daughter, sister, wife, mother, and friend. The large image is from a portrait she had done soon after coming to Washington, D.C., at age 18.

## OH, HOW I LOVE MAMA AND HAIR-DO DAY
**Karen Harting**
*Coppell, Texas*
*49.5" x 75.5"*

**Materials:** *Cotton, Swarovski crystals, metallic threads*
**Techniques:** *Hand and machine appliqué, hand embroidery and quilting*

I was inspired by my mom, Hazel Harting, to create this original design and poem. As long as I can remember Friday has always been hair-do day. Mom got her hair done, and we'd go out for an evening of shopping and fun. For several decades my mom wore the "bee-hive" hair-do and rhinestone cat-eyed glasses. Mom always smells so good that the bees are always around to run from. I hope this quilt blesses her heart and honors her life—*"I love you, Mom."*

## EARTH MOTHER
### Nicole Bridges
*Cordeaux Heights, New South Wales, Australia*
39" x 51"

**Materials:** *Cotton fabric, some hand-dyed, metallic threads*
**Techniques:** *Fused collage, machine appliqué and quilting*

*Earth Mother* is a tribute to my beloved and dearly missed grandmother, Lorna Elizabeth Cooper O'Leary (1920-2004). The image is adapted from my favorite photograph of her, and depicts her as I like to remember her—the original Earth Mother, holding our world in her strong, capable hands. Mother, grandmother, artist, cook, potter, gardener, quilter—Nan was so many things to everyone who knew and loved her. Nan continues to be my inspiration in life.

## OF LOVE AND LAUGHTER
### Beth Porter Johnson
*Houston, Texas*
39" x 51"

**Materials:** *Cotton fabrics, some hand-dyed and painted by artist, beads*
**Techniques:** *Machine appliqué and quilting, hand embellishment*

To honor my mother, Dorothy "Dot" Chauncey Porter (b1924), I have focused on moments that reflect the love and laughter we have shared. The nesting figures symbolize my mother's life as a young woman, a mother, and a grandmother. Love, strength, and joy are quilted on the faces. Memories from my childhood, from events shared as an adult, and from exchanges between my mother and my son are shown as vignettes on the quilt, including our visits together to the National Gallery and the New York World's Fair; our late night visits with hot tea and cookies; converting my mother's studio to my son's nursery; and my mother introducing him to Paddington Bear.

## AND THERE WERE NO MORE TOMORROWS II
**Gerry Macsai**
*Evanston, Illinois*
*32" x 29"*

**Materials:** *Cotton, silk*
**Techniques:** *Photo transfer, stenciling, handwriting, machine quilting*

My father left Bobt, Lithuania, when he was 15, after his father died, and came to the U.S. to live with an uncle. His mother had insisted he leave before he was 17 so he would not be called into the Tsar's army, since once in the Russian army (Lithuania was sometimes part of Russia), you never got out. His mother, sisters, brothers, their wives and husbands, and all of their children were shot in the nearby forest in 1943 during the Holocaust. The only mementos I have of my grandmother, Brocha Yonkelowitz Markulevic (1876-1943), are one photograph, two letters in Yiddish, and a locket. The Hebrew text, Kaddish, is the prayer for the dead. The background list of names represents a small fraction of the thousands of extermination camps, work camps, and prison camps.

"Bringing a child
into the world is the
*greatest act of hope*
there is."

–LOUISE HART

## A RIVER RUNS THROUGH IT
**Anne Copeland**
*Lomita, California*
12" x 18"

**Materials:** *Cotton*
**Techniques:** *Fusing, hand painting,
machine piecing and quilting*

My mother, Viola Agnes Lloyd Copeland (1921-2002), and I
are sitting on some rocks by a river in Ruidoso, New Mexico,
dangling our bare feet in the river. I am five. As I look back
on this special day, I know that life is like a river. It is always
changing and flowing somewhere else, but remains the same,
for it comes from the same source always. The faces are blank
to remind me that although my mother's life may have flowed
past, I am forever a part of the river that was her life.

## I SAW A ROBIN TODAY
**Sylvia Weir**
*Beaumont, Texas*
45" x 60"

**Materials:** *Cottons, chenille bedspread*
**Techniques:** *Piecing, machine appliqué*

Sighting of the first robin each spring meant that winter was
surely gone. Mom cut and pieced a few of these miniature
Dresden Plates—all by hand from cardboard templates. I finished them and put them together in this piece. I hope she is
sitting in her favorite chair in Heaven, quilting something
special for St. Peter. This quilt was created in honor of my
mother, Viola Schwenn Bartels (1932-2000).

## MEDALLION
### Tuula Mäkinen
*Tampere, Finland*
55" x 80"

**Materials:** *Wool, wool blends, viscose thread*
**Techniques:** *Hand piecing, machine embroidery and quilting*

As a child, I admired the portrait of my mother wearing her wedding dress. The dress no longer exists as she made it into a christening gown, which is passed down in the family. I also remember mother's silver lined medallion. Unfortunately, both the medallion and the photograph were destroyed in a fire. By making this quilt, I wished to bring back the memories of my mother, Irja Vuokko Savijärvi (1915-1995), as it has been a decade since she passed away.

## ALBUM
### Susan Leopold
*Toronto, Ontario, Canada*
9" x 12"

**Materials:** *Recycled goods, fabric, paint*
**Techniques:** *Machine quilting, hand stitching, mixed media collage*

This quilt is a tribute to my grandmother Erna Eichenberg Leopold (1900-1983). She was the strongest and most independent woman I have ever known. I always felt special, valued, and safe in her presence. For me, this photo symbolizes the beauty of the mother/child relationship. Looking at her face I feel love on many levels—my love for my grandmother, her love for her baby (my father Vern), her love for me, and the origins of the love I feel for my two daughters, Rachel and Isabel Fleisher.

## PRESERVING LOVE
### Ann Horton
*Redwood Valley, California*
*53" x 62"*

**Materials:** *Cotton, vintage textiles, rayon threads*
**Techniques:** *Appliqué, machine embroidery, photo transfer*

On our family farm, food represented the cycle of life. Planting, harvesting, and preserving were the seasons we lived. I remember my mother in the garden, at the kitchen sink. With kettles steaming, she produced shelves of canned food, all labeled like those she wrote for this quilt. Her love was constant, and like the food she preserved, we knew she would be there for us in times of need. *Preserving Love* is a tribute to the heart and soul of my sweet and loving mother, Eula Laverne Gaddie Kahle (b1924), as is the poem I wrote on the quilt:

*Heartland Daughter, Farmland Wife*
*Through all the Seasons of life*
*Growing, Caring, Preserving Love*
*The Roots and Fruits of God's Abundant Blessings*

## MOTHER
### Judy B. Dales
*Greensboro, Vermont*
36" x 37"

**Materials:** *Cotton, tulle, cotton back*
**Techniques:** *Machine piecing, quilting, and appliqué*

My mother, Narcissa Cameron Boyd (1916-1990), has been gone for 15 years, and I miss her more every year. My mother was not perfect, but her love for me was. That is a gift every child should have, a gift that is carried into adulthood and sustains you every day. The drawing for this quilt has been in my files for quite some time. It always said "mother" to me. The shapes in the center of the design evoke the quintessential image of motherhood, the Madonna. The overall design is abstract but calls to mind the qualities associated with motherhood: warmth, protectiveness, and tenderness. The central figure is surrounded by clouds of curving shapes suggestive of being encompassed, gathered in, loved, and nurtured.

### HEART BROKEN
**Catherine Lombardi**
*Contamine sur Arve, France*
*31" x 43"*

**Materials:** *Cottons, batiks*
**Techniques:** *Machine appliqué, piecing, and quilting*

I remember Mama, heartbroken. Alcohol and its diabolical spiral converted my mother, Françoise Nassif (b1930), into this terrifying monster. Which one of us had her heart broken by the never-ending chain of glasses? It is your wrath and it is mine which streak my picture like lightning, and spin the spiral of your fall into that of my grief. Here we are, together for once, in what I never could tell you before.

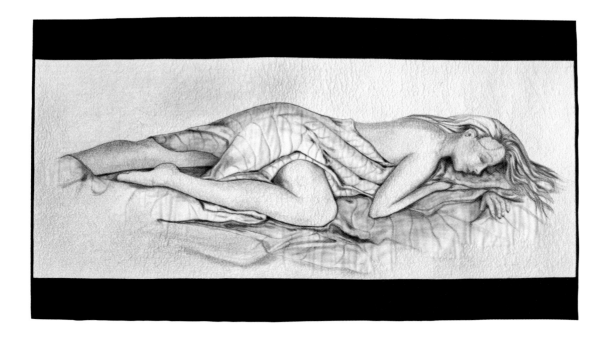

## MY SLEEPING BEAUTY
**Susan Lewis-Storey**
*Austin, Texas*
56" x 30"

**Materials:** *Cotton*
**Techniques:** *Hand painting for sketch, machine quilting*

Many a mother has gazed upon her sleeping child and basked in the maternal miracle of birth and innocence. My first born, Laurie Denise Young (b1976), is depicted here at 29, wrapped only in her mother's quilt, and symbolically represents the sweet innocence that I, as mother, always embrace in my children no matter their age.

## LESSONS LEARNED
**Marlene Linton O'Bryant-Seabrook**
*Charleston, South Carolina*
43" x 33"

**Materials:** *Cotton, African prints, metallic quilting thread, heirloom embellishments*
**Techniques:** *Machine piecing and quilting, photo transfers, embellishment*

This tribute in fabric focuses on five lessons modeled by my phenomenal grandmother—Fannie Rutherford Greenwood-Quarles (1895-1980)—and learned by my mother—Arabella Greenwood Linton (1916-1996)—who passed them on to me, her only child. Through my ancestors, I have learned about the gift of legacy, the rewards of educating, the fulfillment of creating, the flair for fashion, and the serenity of "letting go." The primary color of this tribute in fabric was chosen to honor my Greenwood legacy.

## WAVES OF MEMORIES
**Olena Nebuchadnezzar**
*Virginia Beach, Virginia*
48" x 32"

**Materials:** *Cotton, silk, cotton and rayon threads*
**Techniques:** *Painting, dyeing, appliqué, machine embroidery and quilting*

The quilt is constructed of 70 squares representing the 70 years my mom, Inessa Gusarenko (b1934), has lived so far. The wavy edge symbolizes the infinity, as I wish her to live endlessly. Early years of her life are shown in black colors for they were saddened by the war, famine, and death when she lived in Ukraine (then part of the USSR). Plants, birds, and fish symbolize her great love of gardening. Wherever she lives, she manages to grow marvelous gardens no matter how small the place.

"Motherhood:

*All love begins*

and ends there."

—ROBERT BROWNING

## SHE CAN BAKE A CHERRY PIE
**Madeline K. Hawley**
*Athens, Georgia*
*26" x 30"*

**Materials:** *Cotton, fused vinyl, antique handkerchief*
**Techniques:** *Fusing, machine appliqué and embroidery*

She could bake a cherry pie, or apple, peach, blackberry, or pumpkin. Mama—Nola Williams Crane (1910-2005)—was a pie maker extraordinaire. When my first pie-making effort resulted in a sunken, misshapen lump in the bottom of the pan, she taught me her techniques, right down to measuring salt in my palm. We never had a family dinner that didn't include at least two of Mama's luscious pies, usually topped by a generous scoop of ice cream.

## MY MOTHER, MY MUSE
### Karla Thomas Solomon
*Vienna, Austria*
22" x 27"

---

**Materials:** *Cotton, some hand-dyed*
**Techniques:** *Fused appliqué, piecing, machine quilting*

---

My love of fabric and art comes from my mother, Josephine Phillips Thomas (1927-1999). Sometime in the 1960's she painted this picture, which hung on the kitchen wall all through my childhood in Grant, Michigan. My mother died in 1999, so I can't ask her the story behind it, but I've always believed it to be a picture of her holding me, her last baby. Reinterpreting her painting in fabric has been a moving experience, connecting me to her in yet another way. If it wasn't the two of us in her picture, it is in mine.

## SUMMER DAYS
### Pamela Day Puckette
*Encinitas, California*
27" x 26"

---

**Materials:** *Cotton, cotton threads, hand-quilted cotton remnants*
**Techniques:** *Collage, hand and machine sewing and quilting*

---

Summer Days represents 1950's summers in Tucson, Arizona with my grandmother—Anna Walker Day (1898-1973)—the quilter whose remnants are included in my collage. Grandma Day endlessly worked as she ironed, sewed by hand, and baked incredible peach pies. I remember cross-country trips on Route 66, the desert and the mountains, hula hoops, donuts baked by Grandpa Day, late nights at the drive-in, and snippets of love like the snippets of quilts left to me by the remarkable Anna Day.

## MOM ON VACATION
### Margaret A. Phillips
*Cos Cob, Connecticut*
14" x 21"

**Materials:** *Cotton, some hand-dyed, cotton and polyester threads*
**Techniques:** *Machine appliqué, embroidery, and quilting*

This is my mom, Frances Urban Phillips (b1929). She and my dad, John Phillips, had six children. I am the second oldest. My dad took this picture while they were on vacation in Aruba. It was a sunny day, and she looks like she is having a good time. I like making pictorial quilts; using the quilting to enhance the shading was my biggest challenge.

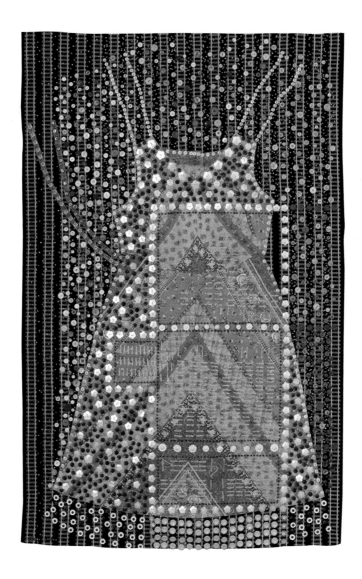

## HOPE DIES LAST
### Rachel Roggel
*Rehovot, Israel*
39" x 60"

**Materials:** *Buttons, mother-in-law's dress, railway fabric, 400 buttonholes, glass beads*
**Techniques:** *Hand sewing, hand quilting through beads and buttons*

On January 20th 1988, my beloved mother-in-law Rivka Tauber Weiss (1928-1988) was laid to rest. It was a rainy day but the sun came out between the clouds. That was the essence of her—even on the gloomiest day she tried to smile.

In 1944, on her 16th birthday, Rivka was transported from Kluj, Hungary, to the infamous Auschwitz-Birkenau death camp in Poland. At the gate, her parents were immediately sent to their deaths. She was left with nothing but the dress she was wearing and hope. On May 9, 1945 she was released and lived to see the railway to the camp covered with weeds and flowers.

On the quilt are 400 yellow buttonholes cut into a dress of Rivka's. They form a blueprint of Auschwitz-Birkenau. Each of the buttonholes stands for a barrack representing the hurt, the tear in the fabric of society. You can never entirely "fix" or bring closure to a buttonhole. It's always there...just as the trauma and the memories were always with Rivka, who never gave up hope.

## MY MOTHER BEFORE ME
### Lesley Riley
*Bethesda, Maryland*
38" x 47"

**Materials:** *Cotton, silk, metal eyelets*
**Techniques:** *Enhanced photo printing on inkjet printer, raw edge appliqué*

They're all tied together—the stories of my mother before me. A lifetime is really a series of moments held together by threads of memory. I know all about the 52 years of my mother's life after I was born, but what about her first 27? The quilt chronicles my mother's journey from little girl to young woman. If every picture tells a story, then this quilt speaks of the life lived before she became my mother—June Proffit Jackson (b1921). Tying the quilt squares seemed appropriate because of all the associations we have with ties: the ties that bind, apron strings, heartstrings, tie the knot, and umbilical cords.

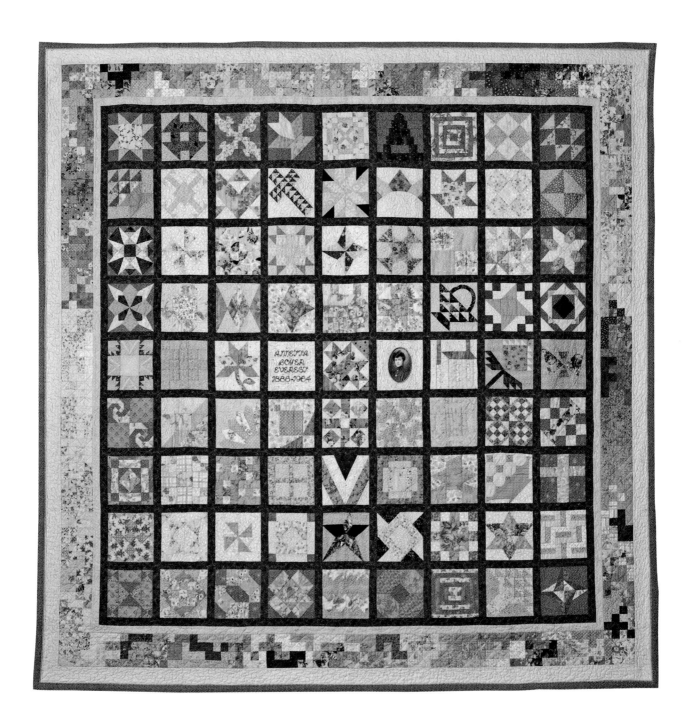

## GRANDMA NETTIE
### Vicki L. Miles
*Osceola, Indiana*
*78" x 78"*

**Materials:** *173 cottons*
**Techniques:** *Electric Quilt 5, BlockBase, machine piecing, embroidery, and quilting*

My Grandma Nettie—Annetta Boyer Everest (1886-1964)—taught me to crochet, knit, embroider, cross-stitch, tat, and sew. She planted and watered my love of the needle. Grandma died when I was 13 years old, but her love of God and her love for me have always been lights in my life. I designed this quilt with one pieced block commemorating each year she lived, and I used blocks originally published in that year. They appear in order by year (upper left is 1886; lower right is 1964) with her engagement picture on the front and her 50th anniversary picture on the label.

## HUMBLE STAR—PROUD STAR
### Klara Schäfler-Landsberg
*Haifa, Israel*
58" x 40"

**Materials:** *Hand-dyed cotton, natural flax, computer-printed fabric*
**Techniques:** *Painting, stamping, machine piecing and quilting*

I grew up in the shadows of the Holocaust. My late mother, Roza Altman-Schafler (1922-2000), was a Holocaust survivor. She constantly relived the horrors and spoke about the 148 individuals of our extended family including two of her children—my brothers—who perished. For years I used to listen to her horrible memories over and over again; those stories haunted me in my dreams. One day, my mother made me promise "never to forget" the men, women, and children who were forced to wear the yellow star and who never returned from hell. I was also to remember those few (six family members) who survived and fulfilled the dream to immigrate to Israel and stand proudly under the blue star. Mama, I have kept my promise to you by making this quilt and dedicating it to you and the 148 members of our family who perished. God bless their souls.

"No influence is *so powerful as* that of the mother."

—Sarah Josepha Hale

## NO CHICKENS IN THE GARDEN!
**Linda S. Schmidt**
*Dublin, California*
*35" x 32"*

---

**Materials:** *Cotton, some hand-dyed, fabric paint, puff paint*
**Techniques:** *Machine and hand appliqué, fiber etched trees, hand painted figures*

---

Grandma (Lucia Janet Barr Cavanaugh, 1894-1995) and Grandpa had a farm in South Dakota with a red barn, silver cupola and weathervane. I distinctly remember Grandma, the garden, and hundreds of baby chicks; but Mama—Alice Belle Cavanaugh Evanick, (b1924)—says that she remembers, *"The garden was fenced, and the chickens were not allowed in. If one got in, one of us kids was sent to chase it out."* Here are Grandma, Mama, and I—and one of the chickens sneaking in. Somebody better chase it out!

No matter how old
a mother is,

*she watches*
her middle-aged children
for signs of improvement.

- FLORIDA SCOTT-MAXWELL

## MOM'S 60TH BIRTHDAY MUSE
### Lisa M. Corson
*Bristol, Connecticut*
*22" x 31"*

**Materials:** *Cotton, silk, velvet, ribbon, buttons, charms*
**Techniques:** *Hand and machine quilting, fused appliqué, thread painting, photo transfer*

In addition to being the primary caregiver for my father, who was ill with diabetes, my mother raised a family and worked full time. Later, she left everyone behind to move to Arizona so my father could have better care and a longer life. Two years after moving, my father died, and my mother, Rose Ann LaBonte Plihcik (b1943), was left alone to start her life over. I made this quilt in honor of her 60th birthday, to celebrate her interests, strengths, and quirks. I hope her muse will encourage her to pursue her dreams, appreciate life, and remind her not to take herself too seriously.

## MOTHER COURAGE
**Christel Rebuschat**
*Berlin, Germany*
26" x 33"

**Materials:** *Silk, cotton, wool*
**Techniques:** *Appliqué, machine sewing, hand quilting*

In November 1943, Berlin experienced the heaviest bombardment of World War II. At the same time my brother and I were born in a bunker. For my mother, Erika Müller (d1995), it was a very dangerous situation. It is due to her strength, and the support and love of our grandmother, that we are alive. It is never easy to give birth to twins, but how hard must it have been for my mother, in a bunker, during the bombing?

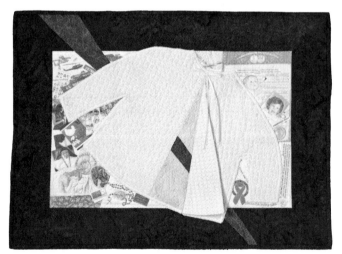

## THE YELLOW SWEATER
**Cheryl Gerhart**
*Churchville, Virginia*
35" x 24"

**Materials:** *Cotton, treated printer fabric sheets, beads*
**Techniques:** *Machine piecing, appliqué and quilting*

On November 17, 1969, my baby daughter was born. I was 18, an unwed mother. I sadly gave her up for adoption, hoping she would have a better life. I crocheted a yellow sweater for her so she would know I loved her. I missed her terribly. On November 1, 1997, I was reunited with my daughter, Suzanne Fetters. She was never given the yellow sweater. The symbolic sweater on the quilt is made of fabric, actually yellow seersucker, which I quilted to look similar to crochet. I made this piece partly as a way to work through my own emotions. When I showed the quilt to Suzanne, I was surprised that she was very moved by it. She held me tight and cried. I do think she knows how much I love her. We now look forward to the rest of our lives as mother and daughter.

### FIRST GRANDCHILD
**LaRetta Ann Trower**
*Smithfield, Virginia*
*44" x 36"*

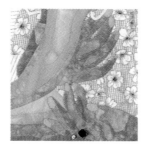

**Materials:** *Cotton, some hand-dyed, metallic and rayon thread, mother-of-pearl buttons*
**Techniques:** *Fused appliqué, free-motion quilting, thread painting for hair and facial features*

As a military family, my husband, Larry, and I often lived in remote places. My mother—Ara Belle Brown Jennings (1920-1993)—saw her first grandchild—Tara Ayanna Trower (b1970)—for the first time when she was one year old. *First Grandchild* portrays that homecoming and was taken from a home photo. The quilt evokes vivid memories of Mama's fabulous flowers and the garnet ring she wore. My memories of her are precious.

"A mother's arms are made *of tenderness and* children sleep soundly in them."

—VICTOR HUGO

## KOUKLA & YAYA
### K. Velis Turan
*Earlton, New York*
*26" x 40"*

My friend, Keith (Koukla), and my Greek mom (YaYa) are together in our back yard on a beautiful, warm summer day with zinnias in full bloom. Keith is dressed for the pool, and Mom is dressed for the North Pole. This image of my mother—Stella Vassos Velis (b1921)—will always make me smile.

**Materials:** *Decorator, hand-dyed and painted fabrics, rayon thread*
**Techniques:** *Machine piecing, trapunto, free-motion quilting*

## TREE TOP TEA HOUSE
**Laura Wasilowski**
*Elgin, Illinois*
*37" x 37"*

**Materials:** *Hand-dyed cotton*
**Techniques:** *Fused appliqué, machine quilting*

One of my favorite pastimes as a little girl was to climb trees. The tree was my house with rooms on many levels and a panoramic view of the Rocky Mountains. My mom—Penelope Neumann (1914-1995)—lived in the tree next door. Each day at 4:00 in the afternoon, she served tea and cookies on the second branch from the top. She always knew how to brew a high spot of green tea.

### GRANNY
**Niki Valentine Vick**
*Austin, Texas*
*28" x 35"*

**Materials:** *Cotton, some hand-dyed*
**Techniques:** *Raw edge appliqué*

Jean Baird Pugh (1891-1991) was a gentle soul and my beloved grandmother. She was always the one I could call on or turn to when I felt things were not going right in my world. Born in 1891, she saw many changes in the 20th century and died quietly in 1991, a month past her 100th birthday. This quilt portrait, taken from a charcoal sketch when she was 80, was created using techniques learned from Marilyn Belford.

## CLARA'S QUILT
### Claudia B. Wood
*Senoia, Georgia*
*37" x 50"*

**Materials:** *Cotton, antique lace, photo transfer fabrics*
**Techniques:** *Machine piecing, three-dimensional appliqué, photo transfer*

This quilt honors my late mother, Clara Addicks Boykin (1912-1983), and my favorite poet, Emily Dickinson. Photos are of my mother, her belongings, or items that represent her talents. The words are a reversal of Emily's poem, *I'm Nobody,* speaking to the issue of self-esteem, which is a struggle for so many women. The budding tree, leaves, and flowers represent the hope and potential within us all.

## ERZULIE DANTOR
### Michele David, M.D.
*Chestnut Hill, Massachusetts*
*35" x 39"*

**Materials:** *Batik, cotton, acrylic paints, embellishments*
**Techniques:** *Machine piecing, appliqué, and quilting*

I made this quilt in honor of my mother and was inspired by Erzulie Dantor, a Petwo Divinity from the Haitian Voodoo pantheon. She is the Goddess (Loa) of love and motherhood. She is a hardworking, fiercely protective mother.

My mother, Aline Cantave David (b1925), is a widow who reared four young children by herself, in Haiti. I remember how fiercely she protected us and reared three feminist daughters despite living in a very patriarchal society. When I came to the U.S. for college, her encouragement ensured my success.

## BEDTIME
**Sarah Ann Smith**
*Camden, Maine*
49" x 42"

---

**Materials:** *Cotton, synthetic sheers, pajama remnants, textile paints*
**Techniques:** *Hand-dyeing, painting, thread painting, machine appliqué and quilting*

---

Reading to my sons at bedtime is the best part of my day. Since I am the family photographer, there are almost no pictures of me with the boys. I asked my husband to take photos of me reading to the boys so I could make this quilt. The image is a composite of both photos, using Eli's room and Joshua's features. The quilt uses blocks leftover from the quilt for Eli's "big boy bed." If I do nothing else in my life, I want my boys to know how much I love them. They are as essential to life as breathing! I love you, boys! *Love, Mama.*

*Subject of quilt: Sarah Ann Maleady Smith (b. 1957); composite image of her two sons, Paul Joshua Maleady Smith (b1993) and William Elijah Kirkpatrick Smith (b1998).*

## GRAM'S PINK GLASS
**Alice McGunigle**
*Shippenville, Pennsylvania*
54" x 54"

---

**Materials:** *Cotton, rayon and cotton threads*
**Techniques:** *Machine piecing and quilting*

---

I am named after my grandmother, Alice Bridge Staas (1903-1996), and I often recall sitting at her side while she sewed. Sewing and collecting cut glass were her joys. I used a modified Cut Glass Dish block in pink (her favorite color) and quilted it to resemble a piece in her collection. I started this on her 1952 Singer, but soon imagined her saying, *"Why use my old machine when you have a nice, fancy, new one?"*

## MOTHERS AND DAUGHTERS
### Brenda Smith
*Flagstaff, Arizona*
*53" x 38"*

**Materials:** *Cotton, hand-dyed and screen-printed*
**Techniques:** *Screen-printing, ink jet printing, machine piecing and quilting*

My mother died before I was married and had children of my own. I wish that my daughter—Sonja Marlene Smith (b1986)—had the chance to know her grandmother, and that my mother—Sonja Eskola Hale (1929-1981)—could have known me as a mother. These photos are of each of us as young adults (and only as daughters) with our full lives ahead of us. In this quilt, we all come together as mothers and daughters.

## TORTILLAS PARA MAMA
**Sabrina Zarco**
*Little Rock, Arkansas*
50" x 42"

**Materials:** *Beads, buttons, sequins*
**Techniques:** *Machine and hand embroidery, appliqué, beading*

Making tortillas is one of our family's time-honored traditions. Growing into womanhood was not complete without a lesson in making flour tortillas. Grandmother and Grandfather Nunez, who was a wonderful chef, tried to teach me. Then my mother had a try, but somehow my oddly shaped bread never looked as beautiful as the ones shaped by their loving hands. My memories are strong: the sounds of the soft dough patted in their hands, the noise of the rolling pin on the table top, flour everywhere and that wonderful smell. I would pray for help to make my tortillas look pretty so that I could be part of this tradition and one day teach my children how to prepare the food of the Gods. These days I call them creative shapes as I teach my daughter Jessica, my son William, and my grandson Domenic, the tradition of lovingly made warm tortillas.

## AUNT DORA, MY MOTHER, AND ME
**Martha E. Gimenez**
*Boulder, Colorado*
16" x 39"

**Materials:** *Batik, cotton, family heirlooms,*
*including mother's unfinished needlepoint*
**Techniques:** *Free-motion machine quilting, appliqué, collage*

Aunt Dora was my mother's favorite sister. I remember them laughing, playing cards, reminiscing about their youth, sharing stories about past pleasures, lost loves, and unfulfilled dreams. They let me play with their furs, wear their perfume, and try on their hats and shoes. I adored them. After their death, I mourned the wise, loving women they had become and the charming girls, full of hope, that they once were. Remembering my mother, Angelica E. Ribo de Gimenez Rossi (1908-1998) and my aunt, Dora Ribo de Cajal (1898-1984).

## MAMMA MIN (MY MOTHER)
### Kolla Bunch
*London, United Kingdom*
*30" x 39"*

**Materials:** *Fabrics, some painted, silk-screened, mono-printed*
**Techniques:** *Mixed*

My mother's life is really all about family. She was the primary caregiver to us. For many years, she took care of my father during his long illness, forsaking all her own interests. A few years back, when she suffered a stroke, it was shocking to realize that we had never thought she could become ill. After all, she was, and thankfully still is, our tower of strength. I have so many wonderful and happy childhood memories, thanks to my mother, Margret Jensdottir (b1934).

2004

# I REMEMBER *Mama*
## MY MOTHER, MY FAMILY, AND ME

## MAGIC CARPET RIDE
**Amy Stewart Winsor,**
**Christine Clarkson Stewart (b1930)**
*Cary, North Carolina*
*34" x 35"*

**Materials:** *Dressmaker fabrics, recycled, hand-painted,*
*and fancy fabrics*
**Techniques:** *Hand and machine stitching, embellishment*
**Family Members:** *Daughter, mother*

Starting with a quilt top made by my mom in the 1980's, I added embellished squares of frayed fabrics. My happiest memories of childhood are the hours I spent reading. I am thankful for my mother's willingness to provide me with library books by the hundreds. Because this quilt reminds me of a Persian carpet, the title, *Magic Carpet Ride*, refers to the way that reading those books carried me away to far-off lands.

## SUNBONNET SUE'S GARDEN
**Joyce Goodson, Lena Karriker Duncan
(1911-1994)**
*Frisco, Texas*
76" x 91"

**Materials:** *Cotton fabric, beads, faux fur, laces, silk ribbon*
**Techniques:** *Appliqué, embroidery, hand quilting*
**Family Members:** *Daughter, mother*

My love of quilting grew from my mother's love of sewing. She passed away in 1994, having started this quilt, which was mostly finished except for one of the blocks. I wanted to honor her and her lifetime of sewing and quilting by finishing this quilt for her, especially since she was such a big influence in my love of quilting.

## PINWHEEL
### Joyce Schnepf, Rose Hodapp Langenhorst (1893-1963)
*Racine, Wisconsin*
43" x 43"

**Materials:** *Vintage cotton prints from the '30s, '40s, and '50s*
**Techniques:** *Hand and machine piecing, hand quilting*
**Family Members:** *Granddaughter, grandmother*

In 2002, I found a box of my grandmother's unfinished quilt blocks at my mother's home. Some blocks were lone examples of a particular pattern; others were multiple blocks. When my grandma saw an interesting quilt, she would construct one block to see if she liked it or to remember how to make it. This pinwheel quilt is an example of a multiple block quilt from that treasure box. I took the blocks she had assembled and added a retro fabric border to make this wallhanging.

## OCEAN WAVES
### Jane Elizabeth Carroll Hall, Julia Gosman (b1845), Elizabeth Jane Gosman (1868-1958)
*Raleigh, North Carolina*
65" x 80"

**Materials:** *Cotton*
**Techniques:** *Hand piecing, hand quilting*
**Family Members:** *Great-great-granddaughter, great-great-grandmother, great-grandmother*

My mother gave me this quilt top, which her grandmother had given her. Grandma Gosman, for whom I was named, had in turn been given the top by her mother-in-law, Mrs. Robert Gosman. I was thrilled with the gift and immediately quilted it. The family lived on the eastern end of Long Island, in the Wading River/East Hampton/Amagansett areas, and the pattern and fabrics are typical of the last part of the 19th century.

## IDA—BIO-IMAGERY: THE KINDNESS OF STRANGERS
### Susan Lewis-Storey, Lydia Murphy Lewis
*Austin, Texas*
*30" x 23"*

**Materials:** *Fabric, thread, Prismacolors, digital photo collage*
**Techniques:** *Hand-coloring, hand-painted watercolor-digitized, beading, machine piecing and quilting*
**Family Members:** *Daughter, mother*

In 1912, my great-grandmother, Ida Rein (1877-1957), was alone, destitute, and unable to find work, food, or shelter. In desperation, she briefly considered drowning herself and her daughters in Galveston's Gulf of Mexico waters. As she walked and prayed for an answer to her plight, a stranger approached and took them to live in her guesthouse. There she found work as a seamstress for the woman and her wealthy friends. The photo collage reveals a life long lived, and descendants who would not have been born and beloved if not for answered prayer and the kindness of strangers.

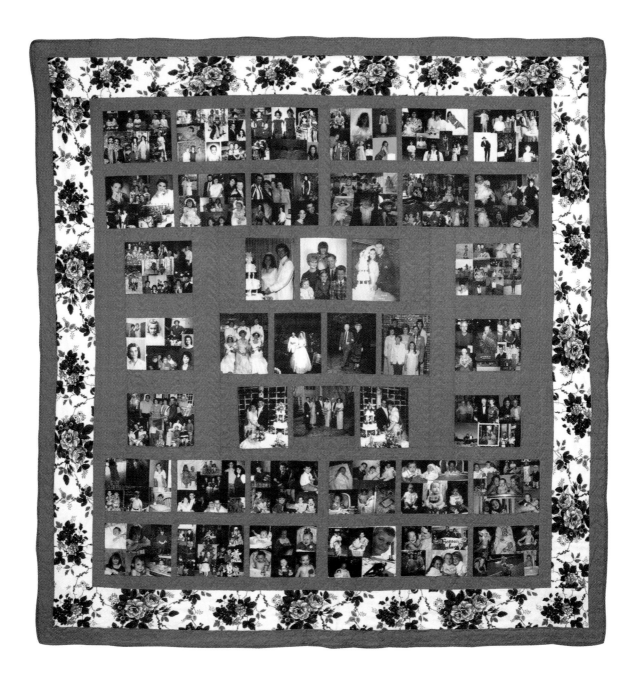

## CROTWELL MEMORIES
**Stephanie LaCour Brian, Melanie Brian Honeycutt, Dana Crotwell Shepherd, Kay Carpenter Crotwell**
*Denham Springs, Louisiana*
90" x 103"

**Materials:** *Sheet, floral print fabric, photograph*
**Techniques:** *Photograph transfer, machine piecing and quilting*
**Family Members:** *Four sisters-in-law*

The quilt was made for my husband's parents, Herman and Evelyn Crotwell. They adopted four children, Pat, Melanie, Ken, and Dana. The family has grown to 31 members. We could not wait for Mom and Dad to open the quilt on Christmas morning.

## I WAS THERE
**Ann Lee, Sonja Lee**
*Lowell, Massachusetts*
45" x 35"

**Materials:** *Painted and printed fabrics, threads*
**Techniques:** *Image transfers, machine quilting, hand embroidery*
**Family Members:** *Daughter, mother*

In this first joint project, Mom and I honor and remember our grandparents: mine—Florence and Leon Older, Dorothy Hedin Ojard; and Mom's—Letty and Gene Hedin, Vivian and Earl Lee. We each created our own composition. Our original intent was to weave the compositions together to symbolize how families' lives intertwine, but we realized precious imagery was lost in the weaving. Instead, we suggested weaving by interweaving checkerboard patterns cut from each composition.

## THE HOME PLACE
**Bernadette Pohl (b1934), Kathy Finley, Karen Hampton, Janet Becht, Amy Whitesel, Justine Becht, Jasmine Becht, Adam Pohl, Cody Pohl, Tricia Schenk, Grant Becht**
*Ft. Branch, Indiana*
30" x 21"

**Materials:** *Cotton fabrics*
**Techniques:** *Machine stitching and quilting, fused appliqué*
**Family Members:** *Mother, three daughters, seven grandchildren*

*The Home Place*, Bernadette Pohl's home since 1957, was built in 1886. It has been more than just a holiday gathering place for her nine children and their spouses, 23 grandchildren, and four great-grandchildren. All ages gather here to learn crafts from marbleizing fabrics to felting. Bernadette, at age 69, made her first wall quilt in collaboration with three daughters and seven grandchildren. It will hang in the home as a reminder of the many blessings shared at *The Home Place*.

"God could not *be everywhere* and therefore he made mothers"

—ANONYMOUS

## THE EVIL EYE
**Janice P. Dawson (b1931),**
**Carolyn Dawson**
*Layton, Utah*
25" x 34"

As my daughter Carolyn and I discussed entering the exhibit, her first comment was, *"Let's do the Evil Eye!"* Reluctantly, I agreed to resurrect a 25-year-old design class project that had morphed into a family joke. The original painting hung on a basement wall for many years where it gazed intently at my six children whenever they used the phone. They eventually dubbed it the "Evil Eye."

**Materials:** *Hand-dyed cotton*
**Techniques:** *Enlarged from original painting,*
*appliqué, machine quilting*
**Family Members:** *Mother, daughter*

## PASSING IT ON
**Margreta Voskuilen Silverstone,
Case Voskuilen, Ada Voskuilen**
*Takoma Park, Maryland*
70" x 73"

**Materials:** *Cotton, threads, ribbon*
**Techniques:** *Machine piecing and quilting, appliqué,
hand embroidery*
**Family Members:** *Daughter, parents*

This quilt represents four generations of our family, four generations of values and beliefs passed down, a Dutch heritage (brought to the United States in 1960), and Calvinistic faith. It represents two generations of quilters. Case and Ada Voskuilen and daughter, Margreta Voskuilen Silverstone, designed and created this quilt together. The team jointly planned the block concepts, the initial layout, and the assembly of the top. Each member created individual blocks within a defined color scheme.

## OUT OF TOUCH
### Pamela Allen, Cecilia Oxley Wright
### (1925-2005)
*Kingston, Ontario, Canada*
*43" x 50"*

**Materials:** *Scrap fabrics, beads, photo-transferred fabric*
**Techniques:** *Hand appliqué, machine quilting, embellishment*
**Family Members:** *Daughter, mother*

I thought when I asked my mother, age 80, to participate in this project, that it would be fun for her. Much to my dismay, making a "family portrait" with the Bubble jet picture I sent caused her great anxiety and sleepless nights. She was worried that it *"wouldn't be good enough!"* Only then did I realize my mother had changed and lacked the confidence she had in her youth. I had lived in another city from my mum for most of my adult life and was obviously out of touch with the realities of her life. I felt sad and pictured myself as being very different, "outside," and sort of "pinned in" to the rest of the family.

## FEATHERED FRIENDS
### Nancy Kazlauckas, Agnes Campbell
*Sauk Centre, Minnesota*
*80" x 80"*

**Materials:** *Cotton, embroidery floss*
**Techniques:** *Redwork, thread calligraphy, machine quilting*
**Family Members:** *Daughter, mother*

*Feathered Friends* represents the collective interests and skills of my family. My nature-loving husband has knowledge of and an affinity for birds. My mother, Agnes Campbell, 87, embroidered all the redwork. And I learned pen and ink calligraphy from my father. I recently created the thread calligraphy technique using a regular sewing machine, and that's the method used in the lettering of this quilt.

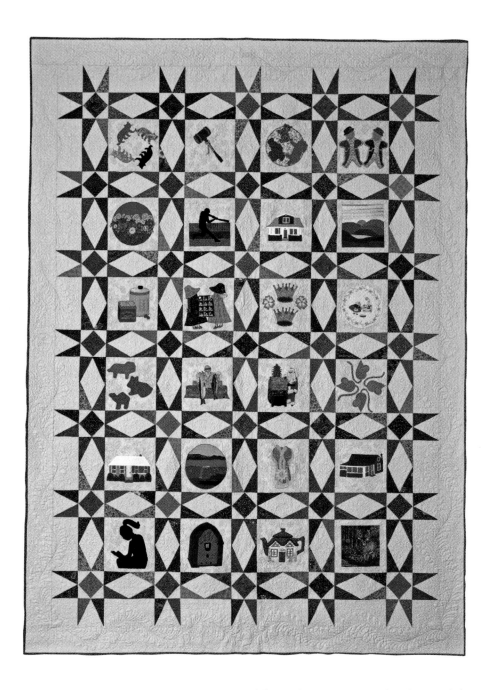

## LIFE'S MEMORIES
**Mary Beth Frezon Goodman,
Elizabeth (Betty) Mulligan Frezon (b1930),
Edward Frezon (b1932)**
*Brainard, New York*
66" x 89"

**Materials:** *Cotton fabrics, polyester sheer*
**Techniques:** *Machine appliqué, piecing, and quilting, fusing*
**Family Members:** *Daughter, parents*

This quilt represents people, places and things important to my mother, me, and our family: mom's childhood home, my parents' home, summer camp, tea and teapots, cats, and other special memories. Quilting is something Mom and I both enjoy and enjoy doing together. We each made blocks (some with Dad's help), planned the quilt, shared the work, and as mom says, "we are still friends."

## FLYING HIGH ON LIFE'S JOURNEY
Meena Manudhane Schaldenbrand,
Shyama Kabre Manudhane (b1936),
Lisa Schaldenbrand, Amy Schaldenbrand
*Plymouth, Michigan*
51" x 64"

**Materials:** *Buttons, charms, fabric yoyos*
**Techniques:** *Beading, embroidery, net overlay*
**Family Members:** *Daughter, mother, two granddaughters*

We are pilots of Life's journey. The airplane's cockpit has our philosophy and Mom's quotes: Attitude (positive), Blessings Counter, Charity, Dreams, Enthusiasm, Family (forget faults), Goals, Humor, Imagine Happiness, Jackpot, Kindness, Love, Music, No Borrowing, Opportunities, Prize, Quilter's Fuel—Fabric and Fun, Recycle, Shopping, Trips, Use Success, Values, Work, Yield, Zone of Traditions. Embellish life and push the right buttons!

## NINE LIVES
### Pat Owoc, Irene Beardwell Cook (b1918)
*St. Louis, Missouri*
45" x 42"

**Materials:** *Antique and new embroidery panels, cotton fabric*
**Techniques:** *Hand embroidery, piecing, quilting*
**Family Members:** *Daughter, mother*

Mom's recent embroidery, three cross-stitched cats, and six of my earliest embroidered cats had decorated tea towels. Now, framed by reproduction 1930's fabric squares, they have become a wallhanging for Margaret, Irene's granddaughter and my daughter. Mom lives in western Kansas and continues to quilt and do needlework.

## GRAM'S NINE PATCH
### Barbara Anne Stewart,
### Mary Elizabeth Durant King (1872-1961)
*Coconut Grove, Florida*
67" x 90"

**Materials:** *Vintage cottons*
**Techniques:** *Hand piecing and quilting*
**Family members:** *Granddaughter, Grandmother*

This was such a wonderful idea. I've been thinking a lot about my gram lately. The last time I saw her was when I left Cleveland for California in 1960. She was knitting up a storm to fill a giant cardboard box with tiny sacques, bonnets, and booties..."*Because so many new babies are coming.*" Gram hand pieced the quilt blocks in the 30s or 40s, and I assembled and hand quilted the quilt much later.

### DAUGHTER'S GIFT
**Ann Kahle Horton, Jessica Horton (b1983),
Eula Gaddie Kahle (b1924)**
*Redwood Valley, California*
48" x 52"

**Materials:** *Cotton, rayon threads, beads*
**Techniques:** *Hand appliqué, machine embroidery, thread painting*
**Family Members:** *Mother, daughter, grandmother*

*Daughter's Gift* began years ago when my daughter, Jessica, then 12, handmade an appliqué Poppy quilt block as a gift to me. The following year she made the Strawberry block. I designed the larger quilt to highlight Jessica's work. As a finishing touch, my mother Eula helped with the hand quilting on Mother's Day, 2004. Sewing and quilting are sweet gifts shared among the women of our family.

## CELEBRATION—A STORY
**Christine Landenburger Adams,**
**Carla Landenburger**
*Rockville, Maryland*
42" x 42"

**Materials:** *Batik fabric and paint*
**Techniques:** *Appliqué, free-motion quilting, ransom note lettering*
**Family Members:** *Two sisters*

My sister Carla and I have always said that we were the best of nine siblings—the oldest and youngest, the alpha and the omega. I laughed out loud when I received the card Carla created for my 50th birthday. Since she is no longer able to do extensive handwork, I adapted the card she made for me as a wall quilt. She designed; I added color and texture. Reading between the lines, it is clear who Carla really thinks is best.

## MAMA'S LULLABY: VARIATIONS ON A THEME
### Beth Porter Johnson (b1950), Jeanette Porter Kiech (b1950), Dot Chauncey Porter (b1924), Jenny Kiech (b1980), Madison Kiech (b1999)
*Houston, Texas*
30" x 43"

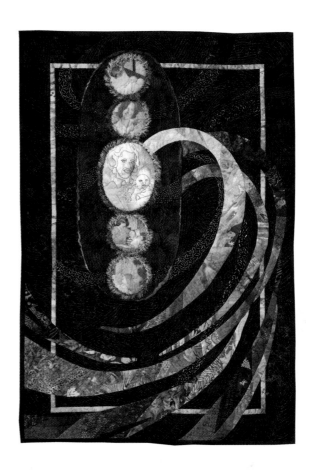

**Materials:** *Cotton fabric, fiber and bead embellishments*
**Techniques:** *Photo transfers, appliqué, machine quilting*
**Family Members:** *Two daughters, mother, granddaughter, and great-granddaughter*

What an awesome moment it is when mothers first hold their babies! In this original quilt design, we—Dot, Beth, and Jeanette—feature the shared experiences of mothers and newborns and also celebrate daughters becoming mothers themselves. During this quilt's construction, our family team of mother and twin daughters expanded to include granddaughter, Jenny, and great-granddaughter, Madison (age 4). Four generations working on this quilt strengthened family ties and added memories full of joy and laughter.

## PRISCILLA'S CALENDAR QUILT
### Leslie Tucker Jenison, Jean Tucker (1925-2003)
*San Antonio, Texas*
51" x 64"

**Materials:** *Cotton*
**Techniques:** *Hand appliqué, hand and machine quilting*
**Family Members:** *Daughter, mother*

My mother hand appliquéd the blocks for this calendar quilt as a gift for my older sister, Priscilla (1947-2001), until she began to experience symptoms of a rare neurological condition. As the disease affected her fine motor skills, the quality of her handwork was affected, and she was unable to complete the project. I made the Postage Stamp borders and did the hand and machine quilting. I was working on this piece at the time of my mother's death.

## OH, THE THINGS WE SAY!!
**Patricia (Pat) Moormann Kumicich (b1947),
Jennifer Ferris Neuman (b1968)**
*Naples, Florida*
*47" x 41"*

---

**Materials:** *Cotton, fabric paints, colored pencils*
**Techniques:** *Machine appliqué, computer-designed fabric,
machine quilting*
**Family Members:** *Mother, daughter*

---

My daughter, Jennifer, introduced me to quilting, so it seemed fitting that we should collaborate on a quilt. We each designed our
self-portraits in machine appliqué. Jennifer designed and pieced
the border and designed the border appliqué. I then completed the
border appliqué and machine quilted the piece. The background
fabric is comprised of things we used to (and still do) say to each
other. It was great fun working together.

"Mother is the name
for God in the
*lips and hearts*
of little children."

–WILLIAM MAKEPEACE THACKERAY

## IDA—STAR
**Susan Lewis-Storey,**
**Lydia Murphy Lewis**
*Austin, Texas*
16" x 16"

**Materials:** *Fabric, thread, Prismacolors, digital photo*
**Techniques:** *Hand-colored digital photo, machine piecing and quilting*
**Family Members:** *Daughter, mother*

A parade photo taken of my great-grandmother, Ida Rein (1877-1957), in the costume she made, served as the inspiration for this quilt. We digitally repeated the whole image of her to form a patriotic star surrounding her face, which we then hand-colored and quilted.

## NANCY
**Frances Holliday Alford,**
**Anne Holliday Abbott, Sallie Holliday,**
**Lily Holliday, Harriet Holliday,**
**Trevor Holliday, Julia Tryk**
*Austin, Texas*
33" x 37"

**Materials:** *Cotton, linen, fabric dyes, markers, paints*
**Techniques:** *Painting, machine quilting*
**Family Members:** *Six siblings and a cousin*

Our mother, Nancy Hayes Holliday (1915-1971), was a brave, adventurous woman. She bore six children in a period of 13 years. She adjusted to a life in Texas after a childhood in New England. She wanted to maximize opportunities for all of us. All six of us plus our cousin, Julia, painted squares depicting our mother and the objects that reminded us of her. Our talents and abilities varied, and our willingness to open old memories took courage. Nancy died at age 55. Her life was not nearly long enough. We miss her.

## DEEP IN THE HEART OF TEXAS
**Karla Fuston Poggen,**
**Helen Perry Fuston (1915-1994)**
*Las Vegas, Nevada*
*67" x 67"*

**Materials:** *Cotton fabrics*
**Techniques:** *Machine piecing, longarm quilting*
**Family Members:** *Granddaughter, grandmother*

Being the only quilter in my family, I received a Lone Star quilt project started by my Texan grandmother before she passed away. With little to go on, I could only guess what she intended her quilt to look like. I added some of my personality by integrating feathers into the design. While piecing her quilt, I constantly thought of her and felt as if we were working on this project together, something we never experienced while she was living.

## CARRIE
### Vaughn Lynn Ransom, Kathy Hoelscher, Carrie Smith Medlock (1863-1956)
*Houston, Texas*
64" x 84"

**Materials:** *Cotton and a variety of fabrics*
**Techniques:** *Appliqué, machine quilting, stippling*
**Family Members:** *Two great-granddaughters, great-grandmother*

The strip center was made 50+ years ago by my great-grandmother. The border, patterned after an 1885 appliqué quilt, was designed and the quilting done by my sister and me.

## GOOD NIGHT, IRENE
### Julaine Lofquist-Birch, Sharon Nuss
*Rockford, Illinois*
34" x 43"

**Materials:** *Hand-dyed, painted cottons, novelty fabrics, embellishments*
**Techniques:** *Free-motion appliqué and quilting, photo transfer*
**Family Members:** *Two sisters*

Lyrics to a song, written as an elderly husband would, honor our beautiful mother, Irene Forsberg Lofquist (1914-1991). A vine with leaves represents the time line of her life, raising eight children. Eight of the hearts represent love. She was a baker, a spoon collector, a proud Scandinavian. The memories are alive, as is the grief we experienced making this quilt. But we know she still watches over us.

## UNFINISHED NO LONGER
**Ann Louise Mullard-Pugh,**
**Helen Sophie Kroll Mullard,**
**Magdalene Reiss Mullard (1888-1973)**
*Las Vegas, Nevada*
62" x 67"

**Materials:** *1930's cotton and muslin, reproduction fabrics*
**Techniques:** *Appliqué of existing patchwork fragments*
**Family Members:** *Granddaughter, mother, grandmother*

My mother, a non-quilter, saved me a box of quilting blocks from my grandmother. Somehow, Mom knew I would become a quilter. Were they experiments that did not measure up to Grandma's standards? Were they orphans from another project? I will never know why Grandma kept them, or why Mom rescued them, but I have made a quilt of the unfinished blocks to honor my grandmother and all the other women who left unfinished projects behind.

## DUET
**Karen Stiehl Osborn, Jeanne Graff**
*Omaha, Nebraska*
42" x 42"

**Materials:** *Paint, beads, yarn*
**Techniques:** *Hand beading, machine couching, hand painting*
**Family Members:** *Daughter, mother*

For the first time in almost 30 years, Mom and I live near each other and can share our lives more intimately. *Duet* is a tribute to that sharing—a blending of our unique personalities and styles. There are traditional aspects merged with contemporary, artistic touches—needle-turn appliqué combined with painted fabric, square blocks set in an irregular quilt arrangement, two generations melded into one quilt.

## LADY BLOOMS
### Tone Haugen-Cogburn, Erin Cogburn
*Maryville, Tennessee*
33" x 39"

**Materials:** *Cotton fabrics, netting, embellishments*
**Techniques:** *Machine piecing and quilting*
**Family Members:** *Mother, daughter*

We wanted to make a quilt that represented each quilter in our family with a flower: "Granny," Hattie Roberts McCammon (1916-2003); two grandmothers, Dorothy McCammon Cogburn (b1937) and Ada Jorgensen Haugen (b1929); and mother and daughter. My daughter Erin, 11, and I each picked our favorite color to work with—yellow and pink—and then added others. Erin did the strip piecing, picked the buttons and beads, and sewed them on. I did all the curved piecing and machine quilting. We had many good talks about these women and made wonderful memories for a young girl.

## SENTIMENTAL JOURNEY
### Jamie Fingal, Jen Fingal
*Orange, California*
20" x 23"

**Materials:** *Fabrics, photo transfer*
**Techniques:** *Fusing, watercolor transferred to fabric, photo transfer, machine quilting*
**Family Members:** *Mother, daughter*

*Sentimental Journey* was a labor of love. I wanted to make a quilt dedicated to my Grandma Alice—Alice Genevra Fletcher Cann (1902-1975)—who taught me how to sew. The legacy lives on in my daughter, Jennifer Alice Susie Fingal, who helped with this quilt. It is based on a photograph of my grandma standing in the kitchen of my early childhood home in Whittier, California. The binding contains a brief history of her life, birth, parents, siblings, marriage, and child. The border is filled with some of my best memories of her.

## LOBSTERS AND SPARKLERS
**Frances Holliday Alford, Anne Holliday Abbott, Sallie Holliday, Lily Holliday, Harriet Holliday, Trevor Holliday**
*Austin, Texas*
*22" x 37"*

**Materials:** *Cotton, fabric dyes, markers, paints, copper tape, tulle*
**Techniques:** *Painting, fused appliqué, satin stitching, free-motion quilting*
**Family Members:** *Four generations*

Our mother, Nancy Hayes Holliday (1915-1971) would have been proud to see so many family members celebrating the Fourth of July together in mid-coast Maine. Aunt Frances set up an art table, and all the family took turns painting and stamping on the squares. Frances and Sallie added the copper tape and striped binding. We are particularly proud of the efforts of the under-five generation who put their greatest efforts into this family reunion quilt.

## SERENDIPITY
### Peggy Kotek, Margaret Rae Steckel Tooma (1920-2002)
*Madison Lake, Minnesota*
*50" x 50"*

**Materials:** *Cotton*
**Techniques:** *Hand appliqué and quilting*
**Family Members:** *Daughter, mother*

Twenty-some years ago, mom and I decided to collaborate on a project for the boys' weddings. Mom had never made a quilt before, but she studied fashion design in New York, was very talented at choosing fabric, and had a true passion for hand-work. The 30 blocks were tucked away until I put the last few quilting stitches in just a week before our 35th anniversary; that would please Mom, who was a "stand by your man" kind of woman. The setting is "Mother's Valentines," another coincidence. Now I can finish my remaining projects by machine, but this is the quilt that set me free from the safety of tradition so I could embrace change—one stitch at a time.

## LITTLE TREASURES
### Sue Dennis (b1955), Rita Dennis (b1977), Sally Dennis (b1979)
*Sunnybank, Queensland, Australia*
*40" x 47"*

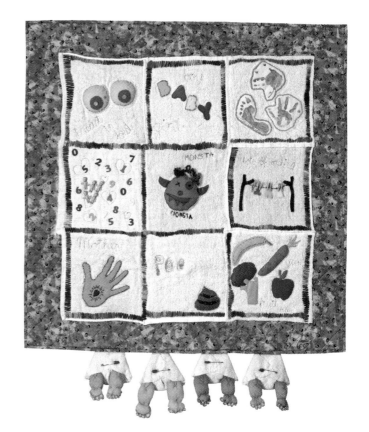

**Materials:** *Cotton, nappies (cloth diapers), felt*
**Techniques:** *Embroidery, hand appliqué, machine quilting*
**Family Members:** *Mother, two daughters*

Babies are beautiful—they are "little treasures." This quilt is a whimsical look at babyhood through the eyes of Sally, new mum of Marli (b2002); her sister, Rita, who is an aunt to nephew, Marli; and Sue, their mother and now a grandma. We wanted to express the joys, surprises, and increased workload of parenting. We hope our quilt brightens your day and brings back memories.

## THERE BE DRAGONS
**Patricia Marie Truitt Mayer,
Nina Marie Mayer Olson,
Chelsea Marie Autio**
*Houston, Texas*
39" x 44"

**Materials:** *Cotton batiks, glass and crystal beads*
**Techniques:** *Hand appliqué, beading, hand and machine quilting*
**Family Members:** *Mother, daughter, granddaughter*

When ancient mapmakers charted an unknown area on their maps, they wrote: "There be dragons." The quiltmaker mother, embellisher daughter, and designer granddaughter (age 15) are linked most closely by our artistic talents. Our husbands, fathers, and brothers are all scientists, engineers, and math lovers. They consider intuition and creative art on the edge of the world they know best. Therefore, we "be dragons" when we are being most creative and intuitive.

## SWEET DREAMS TO THE HOPE OF THE FUTURE
**Joy Finley Palmer,
Lois Burnside Finley (b1923)**
*San Jose, California*
43" x 49"

**Materials:** *Cotton fabrics*
**Techniques:** *Piecing, machine appliqué, machine quilting*
**Family Members:** *Daughter and mother*

I carried my sewing machine from California to a South Carolina nursing home so my mother could help me make a two-generation baby quilt for a future grandchild. We attracted lots of positive attention from fellow patients, staff, and visitors. My mother kept saying, "I really can still do something!" Mama sewed and finger pressed the "star" and "arrow" rows. I made the other rows and finished the quilt. What fun!

A mother laughs our laughter,
Sheds our tears,

*Returns our love,*
Fears our fears.
She lives our joys,
Cares our cares,
And all our

*hopes and dreams*
she shares.

- JULIA SUMMERS

## TRES MUCHACHAS
**Julie Schlueter (b1958), Lauren Schlueter (b1990),
Leah Schlueter (b1993)**
*Orange, California*
*17" x 43"*

**Materials:** *Cotton, netting, yarn, fabric flowers*
**Techniques:** *Piecing, fused appliqué*
**Family Members:** *Mother, two daughters*

My two daughters and I collaborated on this quilt. We each picked the fabric that represented our figure and put the design together. We are swathed in the netting, binding our hearts together forever.

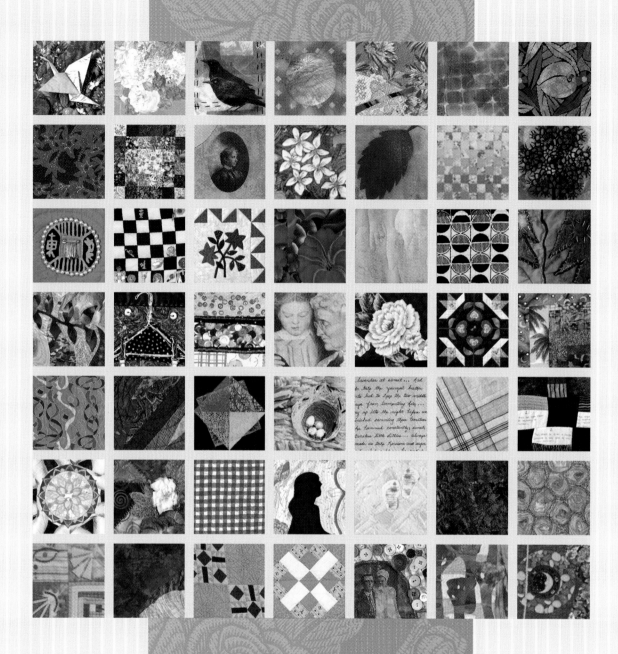

2003

# I REMEMBER *Mama*
### THE HAND THAT ROCKED THE CRADLE

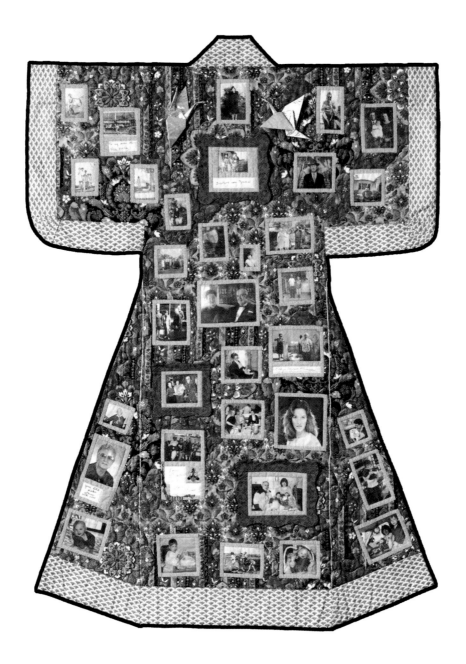

## HAPPY 80TH BIRTHDAY, MAMA
### Sarah Ann M. Smith
*Friday Harbor, Washington*
43" x 60"

**Materials:** *Cotton, gold lamé, fusible web*
**Techniques:** *Machine appliqué, photo transfers, origami,
machine quilting*

Mom's 80th birthday called for something special, so I decided to make a memory quilt for her. I asked my aunts to send me photos of them with Mom when they were kids and adults and to share a favorite memory. Aunt Mary found Mom's old WACS uniform patch and a bracelet Mom gave her from the 1939 New York World's Fair. Aunt Donna sent photos also on behalf of their late brother, Mark. I selected the kimono shape because Mom lived in Japan, fell in love with the people and culture when she served there in 1946-47, and took me there to visit in 1996. I created a stitch depicting lightning and thunder because the Japanese consider them to be holy, purifying elements. The origami cranes represent good luck and long life, which I wish for Mom, Antoinette O. Kirkpatrick Maleady (b1918).

## PORTRAIT OF HOMEMAKER AND ARTIST
### Sonia Callahan
*Piedmont, California*
*46" x 60"*

**Materials:** *Silk, handmade lace*
**Techniques:** *Appliqué, embroidery*

Mom's face emerged during a workshop exercise, and thus this quilt began. Mary Margaret Melichar (1905-2002), my mother, emigrated from Czechoslovakia as a new bride, knowing no English. She displayed her artistry in the clothes she made and wore. The fabric of her dress is made from scraps left after making my bridesmaids' dresses 40 years ago. Mom's love of handwork, flowers, and fine fabric is reflected in her portrait.

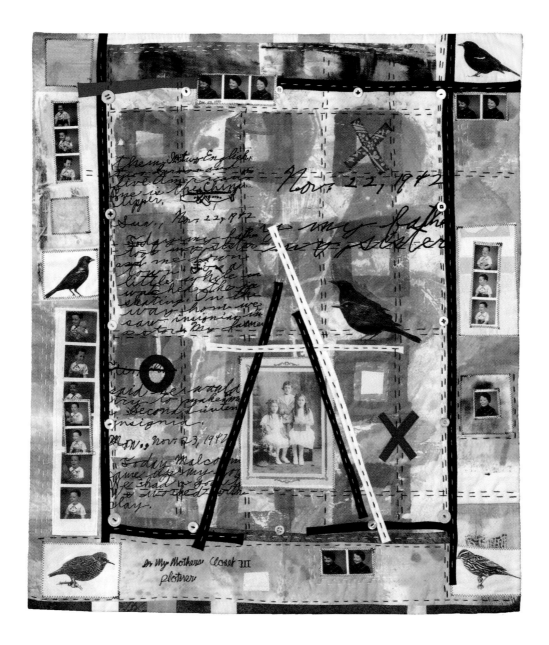

## IN MY MOTHER'S CLOSET III
### Judith Plotner
*Gloversville, New York*
*27" x 31"*

**Materials:** *Cotton, buttons*
**Techniques:** *Silk-screen, dye and paint monoprint, photo transfer*

When I was very young my mother, Sonya Rubin Bernstein (1902-1992), had a divided quilted lingerie box full of treasures in her closet. Every now and then I was allowed to rummage among the Indian head pennies, buttons, photos, and junk jewelry. To me, it was magical. Now that my mother is gone, I found that by recreating memories of my childhood in a series of pieces entitled *In My Mother's Closet*, I could achieve a sense of peace and a connection with my mother who was never too busy and who was always there for me. I reconstructed family life based on things found when we closed up my mother's house: a journal that my brother had written when he was seven; photos of my brother; a photograph of my mother, aunt, and uncle when they were small; birds in memory of my brother's bird-watching days; and tic-tactoe as a general childhood memory.

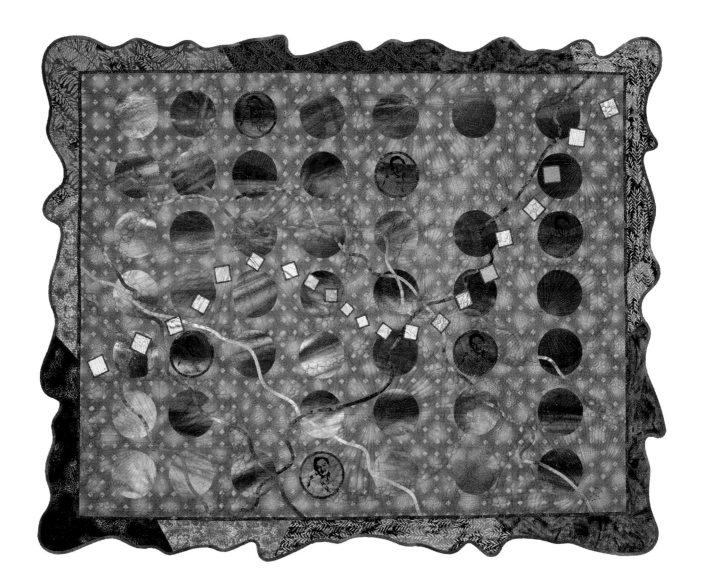

### CELEBRATION OF A LIFE
**Jo Grooms**
*Chelan, Washington*
53" x 44"

---

**Materials:** *Cotton fabric, some hand-dyed, beads, copper*
**Techniques:** *Hand appliqué, silk-screening, embellishment, machine quilting*

---

A mother's love perceives

*no impossibilities.*

— PADDOCK

This quilt celebrates the life of my mother, Virginia Mae Capper Grooms (1918-1971). She died at the age of 52, when I was 16, after a battle with cancer. I tried to convey a happy feeling, without doing an actual portrait. The silk-screen image is from my favorite photo of her, taken when she was young and carefree with her whole life ahead of her.

## PSYCHO-MOMS AT REST
**Katherine L. McKearn and Diane Muse**
*Timonium, Maryland*
*59" x 80"*

**Materials:** *Cotton, vintage potholder*
*and dishtowel, vintage prints*
**Techniques:** *Machine piecing, hand appliqué,*
*embroidery, and quilting*

*Don't bug us.* One of a series.

## PSYCHO-MOMS
**Katherine L. McKearn and Diane Muse**
*Timonium, Maryland*
*61" x 35"*

**Materials:** *Cotton, vintage prints, hand-dyed fabrics*
**Techniques:** *Machine piecing, hand appliqué, hand quilting*

*You think there's a way out but it's really just more of the same.* One of a series.

## PSYCHO-MOMS BAKE A CAKE
**Katherine L. McKearn and Diane Muse**
*Timonium, Maryland*
*80" x 79"*

**Materials:** *Cotton, vintage apron, vintage prints,*
*overdyed and hand-dyed fabric*
**Techniques:** *Machine piecing, hand appliqué, rubber-stamping*

*This is it.* One of a series.

## THE LEGACY
### Liz Berg
*Castro Valley, California*
43" x 49"

**Materials:** *Cotton, silk, paper*
**Techniques:** *Photo transfers, stenciling, photographs, hand embellishment*

My mother, Elizabeth Hollett Smith (1924-2000), lived in Silver City, New Mexico, from age 10 to 14—the happiest years she remembered. Then her father, a cavalry officer, was transferred and a few months later he committed suicide. That act affected my mother deeply, and she wrongfully held her mother responsible. Just a couple of months before she died, she and I revisited her home in Silver City. She was finally able to accept the father she had known as a child as not being perfect and as responsible for his own actions.

## PENELOPE'S PEACHES
**Laura Wasilowski**
*Elgin, Illinois*
*34" x 45"*

**Materials:** *Hand-dyed cotton*
**Techniques:** *Fused appliqué, machine quilting*

My mother, Penelope Neumann (b1914), has a green thumb. One year after canning quarts of sweet peaches, she tossed the peach pits into the garden mulch pile. Five years later, we had a hardy peach tree producing juicy fruit in the backyard. Everything she touched grew.

## MOM
### Suzanne Mouton Riggio
*Wauwatosa, Wisconsin*
13" x 17"

**Materials:** *Cotton, some hand-dyed, silk, tulle*
**Techniques:** *Fusing, painting, machine appliqué*

My mom, Rose Degeyter Mouton (1912-2001), was 80 in this portrait of her sitting on a chair near her back door catching up on the news. In the foreground are St. Joseph lilies, her favorite flower from the garden of her mom, Honorina Castille Degeyter (1874-1955).

## MY MOTHER, MY FRIEND
### Marlene Brown Woodfield
*La Porte, Indiana*
23" x 31"

**Materials:** *Cotton*
**Techniques:** *Hand appliqué, hand piecing, hand and machine quilting, silk ribbon embroidery*

This quilt was a gift to my mother, Ruth Viola Ludders Brown (1909-1995) for her 85th birthday. My hope was that it would convey the love I had for her. Sometime in advance of her birthday, I asked her what she wanted for her birthday. She responded, "A quilt!" At her party, I gave her this Victorian style portrait of herself. She was expecting a new bed quilt, so you can imagine her surprise. She was thrilled.

## THE SEAMSTRESS
### Kim Ritter
*Houston, Texas*
15" x 19"

**Materials:** *Silk, cotton*
**Techniques:** *Pigment dye on silk, machine quilting*

*The Seamstress* is one of the roles that mothers have played in families forever. This seamstress is my Great Aunt Bert—Beatrice Ralls Roberts (1889-1978). She was a professional seamstress by day and made quilts at night for fun. She never sold her quilts, but I am lucky to have inherited one from her. She raised my grandmother (her youngest sister), when the family fell on hard times. Aunt Bert was married to a full-blooded Indian, the Scribe of the Choctaw Nation. Bert loved crystal. As she got older, she always tried to give a piece to whoever came to see her, saying *"I'd rather see your face when you take it; I won't be here to see it when you inherit it."* She was a grand old lady!

## WHEN I LOOK IN THE MIRROR
## I SEE MY MOTHER
**Necia Wallace**
*Whitefish Bay, Wisconsin*
*26" x 28"*

**Materials:** *Cotton*
**Techniques:** *Reverse appliqué, machine quilting*

The older I become, the more I become like my mother, both the good and the bad. I am proud to pass on to my children her willingness to take risks, to try something new, to strive to do the very best you can. Mom's example also inspires me to try to overcome our impatience, our tactlessness, and our failures of understanding. And thank you especially, Mom, for teaching me to sew! My mother was Alma Lippold Patterson (1891-1967).

## JOURNEY TO THE NEXT PLACE
### Debra Wykert
*Muscatine, Iowa*
44" x 44"

**Materials:** *Cotton, Sulky Gold Sliver thread*
**Techniques:** *Strip piecing, broderie perse appliqué, hand quilting*

This quilt symbolizes my mother's life: six butterflies for each member of her family and another outline quilted for her still-born. The colorwash of lights and darks creates a beautiful tapestry that is life—joys and difficulties. The "Breath of God" swirls through in gold quilting, uplifting her to *The Next Place*, much like the book she shared with her grandchildren. The backing, "Tranquil Pond," is my visualization of Heaven. My mother was Charlotte Golliday Brown (1931-1998).

## LOST MEMORIES
### Susan Madden
*Austin, Texas*
22" x 19"

**Materials:** *Fabrics, some hand-dyed and discharged, photo transfers*
**Techniques:** *Machine piecing and quilting, thread embellishment*

My mother, Jeanne Pray Latoszewski Ploger (1916-1998), collected photographs—hundreds and hundreds of photos, over 80 years' worth. Photos she and my father took, photos she inherited from her father, and photos her children took were all meticulously labeled and filed in shoeboxes or carefully glued into neatly labeled albums, all stored in the basement. Her last winter she was too frail to go into the basement where leaking pipes had caused total and heart-breaking devastation. We never told her.

*"All mothers are* physically handicapped. They have only two hands."

—ANONYMOUS

## MOTHER AND I
**Petra Voegtle**
*Munich, Germany*
23" x 34"
From a private collection

**Materials:** *Silk, viscose backing, silk thread, paint, beads*
**Techniques:** *Hand and machine quilting, machine appliqué and piecing, trapunto, painting, beading*

Mother and I is a very personal interpretation of human relationships. It reflects pain and sorrow, a certain helplessness, and the inability to solve the problem. My mother is Ella Astheimer Köntopp (b1927).

## I'M NOT GOING TO BUY ANY MORE PURPLE OR TEAL
**Cherie Ekholm**
*Redmond, Washington*
19" x 21"

**Materials:** *Organza, hand-dyed fabrics, beads*
**Techniques:** *Reverse appliqué, machine quilting, hand beading*

Layers represent the many roles my mother played, the ephemeral nature of life we encountered with her battle with cancer, and Mom's ability to often be there without really being there. The islands of solid fabric represent gardening and the colors she loved. The title phrase is one she uttered every time we shopped for fabric…to no avail. This was the last of my quilts seen by my mother, Judith Kay Jamieson Ekholm (1942-2003).

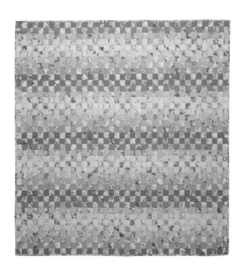

## EARTH QUILT #61: CELEBRATION OF LIFE XIV
**Meiny Vermaas-van der Heide**
*Tempe, Arizona*
58" x 60"

**Materials:** *Cotton*
**Techniques:** *Machine piecing and quilting*

In my Celebration of Life series, I use the tint scale to represent fragility and preciousness of life. These quilts have helped me mourn the loss of children I thought we would never have due to infertility. For me it is true that making art means healing. Despite overwhelming odds, we are blessed with two sons.

## SHE SHOWED ME HOW TO SEE ALL THE COLORS IN THE RAINBOW

**Leslie Tucker Jenison**
*San Antonio, Texas*
*38" x 38"*

**Materials:** *Cotton, rayon and metallic thread*
**Techniques:** *Machine piecing and appliqué, thread painting, free-motion machine quilting*

My mother was a powerful presence in my life. She raised me to believe that women are forces of nature and that I could do anything! She encouraged me to look at challenges from many points of view. Mother lost her battle with a rare neurological disease, but her courage and unfailing sense of humor throughout her ordeal were truly remarkable. I dedicate this work to her, M. Jean Tucker (1925-2003).

## SINGLE PARENT FAMILY
**Pamela Allen**
*Kingston, Ontario, Canada*
50" x 43"
From a private collection

---

**Materials:** *Rayon, recycled fabric, cotton, photo transfer, manufactured items*
**Techniques:** *Raw edge, big stitch appliqué, machine quilting and embellishment*

---

"The mother's *heart is the child's* schoolroom."

–HENRY WARD BEECHER (1813-1887)

A beautiful war bride embraced a hopeful new life in Canada, but four years later, she was abandoned with two little girls. We were a single parent family before the phrase had been invented! Often a sad little unit, we were unsettled by frequent moves, an astonishing sibling rivalry, and occasional separation from each other. My mother, Cecilia Oxley Wright (1925-2005) never gave up on her latch-key kids. She was the pilot who steered us through it all. I love her for it.

### NANA'S GARDEN
**Peggy Kotek**
*Madison Lake, Minnesota*
29" x 13"

**Materials:** *Cotton*
**Techniques:** *Hand appliqué, machine piecing, hand quilting*

This quilt was made in memory of my mother, Margaret Rae Steckel Tooma (1920-2002). Handwork has always been a refuge for me, but lately, driven by deadlines I stitch by machine. After my mother's death, I was unable to grieve until I picked up my handwork and stitched in silence, keeping a journal of my thoughts: *This is the quilt that dried the tears, that held the memories, that healed the pain, one stitch at a time.*

### MOTHER OF LIGHT
**Dara Tokarz**
*Sedona, Arizona*
27" x 21"

**Materials:** *Fabrics, thread, seed beads*
**Techniques:** *Appliqué, beading, free-motion embroidery*

Ideally, most of us learn to love and nurture from our mothers, yet many of us search for the archetype of the ultimate mother who teaches us to love selflessly, to love others as we love ourselves. In Tibetan Buddhism, we find Tara, Mother of Light. Embodied in the face of my spiritual teacher—Jetsunma Ahkon Lhamo (b1949)—Tara teaches us to love.

### MATERNITÉ
**Shelley Dawson Davies**
*Wesley Chapel, Florida*
28" x 28"

**Materials:** *Cotton, satin, lamé, beads, found objects*
**Techniques:** *Photo transfer, quilting, beading*

It takes the patience of a saint to be a good mother, as my own mom, Janice Page Dawson (b1931), so ably proved. Venerating her qualities seems only natural to me now that I have children. What better way to honor her than to pass her qualities on?

## MAMA! DID YOU KNOW...
**Shirley Jo Falconer**
*Hillsboro, Oregon*
15" x 15"

**Materials:** *Fabrics, some dyed, beads*
**Techniques:** *Piecing, appliqué, hand beading*

"*Mama, did you know...*" and my mom would be anxious to hear what I had to say, or she would say, "*Shirley, did you know...*" That was the way we spoke. My mother was Nellie Gottberg Rimkus (1910-1985). During WWII, Mom answered the call to keep the sawmills going; she would stand all day and pull certain sizes of lumber as the wood came from the mill. Years later, I was told that some men don't last a single shift because the work is too hard. Mom did it for nine years...and she milked the cow before and after work, too!

## SPRING CHICK
**Pat Owoc**
*St. Louis, Missouri*
19" x 20"

**Materials:** *Tea-stained cyanotype photograph on cotton, some hand painted fabrics*
**Techniques:** *Cyanotype, painting, appliqué, machine quilting*

This quilt is about Mom, her Leghorn chickens, and her own "Spring Chick"—me—and the Kansas earth that has kept the family going for nearly 65 years. Mom protected her brood, my sister and me, saving us from dangers we saw, like rattlesnakes and pecking geese, and from dangers we didn't see, such as disease, malnutrition, and ignorance. Mom—Irene Beardwell Cook (b1918)—still lives and quilts in western Kansas.

## WHAT MAMA LOVES
**Kimberly Baxter Packwood**
*Ames, Iowa*
12" x 12"

**Materials:** *Cotton, Perle cotton, embroidery floss, glass beads*
**Techniques:** *Kantha style quilting, hand-stitching, beading*

This piece was a real stretch for me. The phrase, "*If you can't say anything nice, then don't say anything at all,*" kept coursing through my head. I can tell you what my Mama—Barbara Kerfont Baxter (1947-2005)—loved: fishin' and campin' and sharing a pot of tea with friends.

## WINDOW TO A MOTHER'S GARDEN
### Shelley Brenner Baird
*Columbus, Ohio*
24" x 35"

**Materials:** *Cotton, embroidery floss, embellishments*
**Techniques:** *Airbrushing, hand appliqué, and hand quilting*

Through a window is the face of a woman, hovering above her children like the sun. Bathed in warmth and light they grow gentle and sweet, hard and strong. With tears, fears, and joy, the mother watches them. She feels powerful and helpless, close and distant.

This quilt is about being a mother and a daughter at the same time. It was inspired by the quilt artist's mother, Barbara Gordon Brenner (b1927).

## WOMAN OF VISION
### Judy B. Dales
*Greensboro, Vermont*
34" x 34"

**Materials:** *Cotton, rayon thread*
**Techniques:** *Machine piecing, hand appliqué, machine quilting*

The quintessential mother is busy, involved, determined, and caring. Her life is a bit frantic, which is reflected by the chaos inside this woman's head. A mother no longer has the luxury of worrying only about herself. She worries about her children and how they will survive in a world damaged by carelessness and conflict. The imagery surrounding the woman reflects her concern for all the living things on our planet. Deeply embedded in the psyche of this woman is the desire for peace, hence the dove holding an olive branch. A mother yearns for peace, not only for herself but also for the children that she has brought into this world.

## HEARTSTRINGS
**Marlene D. Glickman**
*Clearwater, Florida*
*51" x 76"*

**Materials:** *Daughter's clothing and photos*
**Techniques:** *Photo transfers, quilting, fraying*

My daughter, Chehallis Glickman (1970-1994), brought me laughter, friendship and motherhood. When cancer came to her at age 23, I tried once again to give life to her. After her passing, I grabbed at creating something and returned to fabric art. My heartstrings still tug joyfully and tearfully at unexpected times, especially now while making this quilt, using her clothing and jewelry for the hearts, and remembering and writing about our times together.

## BODY IMAGE
### Sabrina Zarco
*Little Rock, Arkansas*
67" x 45"

**Materials:** *Seamstress labels, zippers, lingerie fasteners*
**Techniques:** *Reverse appliqué, embellishment, hand painting*

Grandmother, Rebecca Nunez, and Mother, Naomi Nunez Ybarra, would create personal interpretations of the latest styles. I would sit under the sewing machine gathering bits of fabric, trim, broken zippers, leftover snaps, and buttons. Today these are still the "treasures" I use to create my personal statements. This work is called *Body Image*, something you think about as you are standing on the kitchen chair for just one more fitting before earning the label, *"Made especially for you by Mom."*

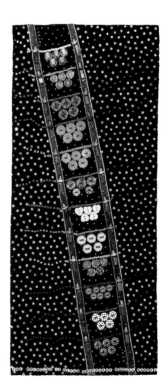

## THE "ALWAYS WEAR CLEAN UNDERWEAR" SAGA
### Rachel Roggel
*Rehovot, Israel*
22" x 24"

**Materials:** *Cotton, buttons, worry dolls, beads, star sequins, silk ribbons*
**Techniques:** *Hand sewing and quilting*

In 1950, my mother, Esperanza (Hope), 14, climbed the airplane's staircase, leaving Iraq for her new country—Israel. Since no suitcase was allowed, she wore all 12 pair of underwear that Grandma Simha (Joy) Maria (1907-1989) sewed especially to assure she wouldn't have to worry about clean ones upon arrival. Today, my family knows that I'll stop any quilt project when the last underwear is announced. In our family, this is one way to say, *"I love you."*

## BURKINABE MOTHER
**Hollis Chatelain**
*Hillsborough, North Carolina*
30" x 42"

**Materials:** *African cloth*
**Techniques:** *Machine quilting*

African babies are never separated from their mothers, which creates a powerful bond that lasts throughout their lives. Before moving to Africa, I had never thought about having children of my own. Our first child was born in a bush hospital in Agou-Nyogbo, Togo. She was delivered by African midwives by the light of a kerosene lamp. This experience and raising our three children in West Africa had a profound impact on my being a mother. I was pregnant with our first child when I photographed this young mother feeding her baby in a market in Burkina Faso. She also represents what I feel mothers do—we balance motherhood with work—and she is accomplishing this in such a beautiful, elegant way.

## MOTHERS/DAUGHTERS #6...LINES OF COMMUNICATION

**Judy Hooworth**
*Terrey Hills, New South Wales, Australia*
*78" x 78"*

**Materials:** *Cotton, blends*
**Techniques:** *Torn and layered fabrics, machine quilting*

Family relationships are fragile at times of stress and emotional upheaval. The bond between mother and daughter is stretched to the breaking point. To help preserve a special and loving relationship, the lines of communication, though tenuous, need to be kept open. This piece emphasizes the complexity of mother-daughter-mother relationships and is part of a series of 10 quilts.

## MOM'S BRIGHT IDEA OF A FRAGILE BALANCING ACT
### Meena Schaldenbrand
*Plymouth, Michigan*
35" x 40"

**Materials:** *Metal pop can tools, charms, trims*
**Techniques:** *Stitching on metal, sheer overlays*

The light bulb represents the bright idea that we mothers can do it all, balancing many roles on life's chessboard, including accountant, banker, cook, cheerleader, driver, gardener, hostess, judge, maid, nurse, photographer, seamstress, teacher, travel agent, waitress, and wife. The tools surrounding the bulb represent exterior pressures. Being a mom is very rewarding, even for a completely unpaid, often underappreciated job! This quilt was inspired by my mom, Shyama Kabre Manudhane (b1936).

## ANNA'S GARDEN
### Marianne Axboe
*St. Louis, Missouri*
18" x 18"

**Materials:** *Cotton, some hand-dyed, sheer fabrics, tatted pieces*
**Techniques:** *Machine piecing and quilting, embroidery, beading*

My mother-in-law's garden was always an explosion of colors featuring many types of flowers and vegetables. She learned to tat and make lace during rehabilitation after polio; the tatted pieces in this quilt are her creations. Remembering Anna Marie Pedersen Nielsen (1926-1997).

## WHITE ROSES ARE FOR MOURNING
**Peggy Daley Spence**
*Tulsa, Oklahoma*
20" x 34"

**Materials:** *Cotton*
**Techniques:** *Fusible appliqué, machine quilting*

Daddy always bought "his girls" corsages for Mother's Day and taught us the code: red flowers for living mothers and white for mothers who had died. This quilt is about the moment I first realized I could never again wear red flowers on Mother's Day. It pierced me. Red roses are for joy; white roses are for mourning. Snowflake prints represent the icy night she died, six years less one day from Daddy's death. Remembering my mother, Joan Wimborough Daley (1919-1997).

## MOTHERING: ADVANCED YEARS
**Sonia Callahan**
*Piedmont, California*
46" x 46"

**Materials:** *Cotton, overlay organza, embroidery floss*
**Techniques:** *Fusing, appliqué, overlay, and patchwork*

This quilt salutes my Mom's love and courage during her life in a care center. It was painful for me to see her in this restrictive environment until I discovered that her life pivoted around food. Not only did food stimulate her senses and nourish her but also meals provided opportunities for socialization and time reference. Mom—Mary Margaret Melichar (1905-2002)—continued to express her love for us until she no longer knew our names, then she pressed our hands with love, and we knew it was the same.

## MY ANGELS
**Myrah Brown Green**
*Brooklyn, New York*
*44" x 54"*

**Techniques:** *Machine appliqué, quilting, embroidery*

My grandmothers—Dora Anderson (1899-1964) and Amy Brown (1913-1996)—have always been my guiding spirits, and my strongest attributes stem from them. Anything that I wanted to try in my life, my grandmothers always made me believe that I could. Quiltmaking takes me through a breathtaking rite of passage into ideas, patterns, symbols, and colorful visions that can be shared with the world. My ancestors stay with me the whole time I work. They remind me of the responsibility I have to those who came before and those yet to come.

## MAMA GOES TO CHURCH
**Madeline Hawley**
*Athens, Georgia*
*29" x 33"*

**Materials:** *Cotton, tulle, antique linen handkerchief, embellishments*
**Techniques:** *Fusing, machine quilting, digital photo*

Above all else, Mother's faith and her church figure most prominently in her life. Her first thoughts in the morning and her last thoughts at night occur with a Bible in her hands. She is entering a church as her favorite Bible passages float around her. Mama, Nola Williams Crane (1910-2005), was 93 when this quilt was made.

## TO EVERYTHING THERE IS A SEASON

**Ann Louise Mullard-Pugh**
*Las Vegas, Nevada*
*61" x 76"*

**Materials:** *Cotton, buttons, embellishments*
**Techniques:** *Piecing, appliqué, embellishment*

Pieced, appliquéd and embellished while I sat with my mother and friend, Helen Sophie Kroll Mullard (1914-2002), who endured Alzheimer's, while being legally blind and profoundly hard of hearing. We talked of gardening, birds, and bugs, holding the same conversation again and again as she could not hold a thought. She did not recognize the embellishments that come from her collection. To everything there is a season; mothers care for their children, and children care for their mothers.

## LISTEN TO YOUR MOTHER
**Jean Ray Laury with machine quilting
by Susani Smeltzer**
*Clovis, California*
36" x 38"
From the collection of the Museum of the
American Quilters Society

**Materials:** *Cotton, paints*
**Techniques:** *Silk screening, hand painting, machine piecing*

I first made this quilt for my granddaughter, Anna Laury, when she went off to college. It was well used and nearly worn out, so I made this similar one. This quilt is about women, motherhood, and me. And you, too. We all pass along, whether intentionally or unintentionally, comments we heard from our own mothers—the wisdom of experience and the warnings of looming dire consequences of any misbehavior. Even when we find the advice somewhat absurd or out-dated, it persists. And one day, we will hear it being passed on to the next generation.

These admonishments ("*I'm telling you this for your own good*") seem universal—"*Watch out, you're going to poke somebody's eye out with that thing*" or "*Put that down—you don't know where it's been.*" I love using words in my quilts, as words capture something essential and personal. Helping the next generation find its way is the goal of the "universal mother."

## ALL MY MOTHERS
### Carole O'Brien
*New Castle, Colorado*
35" x 34"

**Materials:** *Cotton, metallic threads, beads*
**Techniques:** *Machine piecing and quilting, photo transfer, raw-edge machine appliqué*

Central to this piece is my great-grandmother. She is surrounded by five generations, including my adoptive mother, myself, my oldest daughter, and oldest granddaughter. The piece is designed to reflect the connection between women, through the spiral of time, by the mother-daughter bond. As an adopted daughter, I claim all women as my mother. The seasons of my life change, and I move forward in the footsteps of all my mothers before me.

## MISSING ROSE
### Rosanna Lynne Welter
*West Valley, Utah*
60" x 80"

**Materials:** *Fabrics, some hand painted, rayon thread*
**Techniques:** *Monoprinting and machine quilting*

Although I grew up in a family of artists, I was deemed the musical child. While the rest of the family painted, I studied the piano. The shock of my mother's early death, however, precipitated an amazing change of course and a remarkable discovery. My need to remain in some way connected to her led me, in absolute wonder, to realize the artist in me as well. It was a discovery that changed my life.

My mother, Rose Elizabeth Jordan Parke (1920-1984), taught me sewing and instilled in me a love for fabric. Textile/fiber art was my natural choice of medium; it bridged that chasm of grief and connected me to her.

## THERE'S A HOLE IN MY HEART
**Judy Kriehn**
*Garland, Texas*
28" x 30"

**Materials:** *Cotton*
**Techniques:** *String piecing, appliqué*

How do I feel about breast cancer? My mom, Juliette (Julie) Gratke Kriehn (1928-1979) was diagnosed shortly after Betty Ford went public with her battle with breast cancer in 1974, but my mom lost her own battle. I don't know that I appreciated my mom when I was a kid. She wasn't glamorous like the mothers many of my friends had, wasn't much of a cook, and didn't drive a car. With age, I've come to appreciate the many rare qualities she possessed. She taught me that books could take you places you might never visit otherwise. She indulged my vivid imagination. She showed me how to thread a sewing machine, and rarely got mad when I would dismantle all the working parts. She taught me about independence. I learned that people were individuals who deserved respect regardless of their color. She made time for friends and family alike. With her death, I lost someone who for all her faults, was still a pretty amazing role model. There's a hole in my heart that aches as I pass through rites of adulthood that I always thought my mom would be there to see. And that is how I feel about breast cancer.

## WHISPERED SECRETS
**Christine Adams**
*Rockville, Maryland*
16" x 21"

**Materials:** *Cotton fabrics, photo imagery on fabric*
**Techniques:** *Free-motion quilting, appliqué, and computer manipulated lettering*

That there is a special something lingering in the souls of womankind speaks of mystery. In some measure women share in this mysterious quality, and it gives them a feeling of belonging to a sacred sisterhood. *Whispered Secrets* celebrates the beauty, strength, and power of women's relationships to each other. The sisterhood includes any woman who offers love and guidance to the young. My special mentor was my mother, June Kessler Landenburger (1918-1977).

## I STAND ON HER SHOULDERS
**Lyric Montgomery Kinard**
*Cary, North Carolina*
*33" x 34"*

**Materials:** *Cotton*
**Techniques:** *Dye painting, photo-transfer, quilting*

Who am I? Is it only the artist in me, the occupation that is traditionally male, that has value? Does the traditional work done by all those apron-wearing women before me hold value? If I reject as worthless the housework, the child rearing, and the holding of homes and families together, what will become of me? What will become of our children, our society?

In memory of Eliza Groh Yungk, my great-great-great-great grandmother.

## TO MY DEAR MOTHER
**Susan Leopold**
*Toronto, Ontario, Canada*
*5" x 7"*

**Materials:** *Cotton, beads, recycled items*
**Techniques:** *Hand stitching, painting, collage*

*To My Dear Mother* is about my emotions as both a mother and a daughter. The objects and imagery in my quilt are connections between conscious and unconscious, past and present. I collect and save things that I am drawn to. The objects in this quilt have been in my studio for a few years. My process is intuitive, and I work in both layers of memory and material. Memories of my mother, Shirley Bloom Leopold (b1934) and my two daughters, Rachel (b1993) and Isabel (b1996) Fleisher led to the creation of this quilt.

## MARVELOUS MIDGE
**Jeri Riggs**
*Dobbs Ferry, New York*
*30" x 28"*

**Materials:** *Cotton, rayon and cotton thread, glass beads*
**Techniques:** *Inkjet photo printing, machine piecing, embroidery, quilting*

*Marvelous Midge* is my mother, Margaret Wintestone Riggs (b1930). Her alpine rock garden is legendary, comprised of rare plants from all over the world. Edelweiss, campanulas, gentians, and iris grow happily in the rocky outcropping near her house—despite visits from the nibbling deer. I most admire her for going back to school, getting a degree in Human Genetics, and working as a genetics counselor for the past 35 years. She traveled the world with my dad and loves Egypt and Wales. The castle represents her courage in facing the unknown; flanked by her cats, she goes forth into the future.

## THE WHISPERS I HEAR
**Teddy Pruett**
*Lake City, Florida*
*61" x 62"*

**Materials:** *Deteriorated antique quilt,
1940's curtain, vintage crochet*
**Techniques:** *Hand written stories, hand and
machine appliqué*

My thoughts often dwell on the anonymous quilt artists of the past—women whose only legacy is the quilts they left behind. No one even remembers who they were. The women of my family were much the same—intelligent, wise in the ways of the world and nature, but lacking formal education. (My "uneducated" grandmother could translate Latin!)

I lost several of them in rapid succession, and my grief was overwhelming. I could not sew for crying. This quilt is for and about all the women in my family—most specifically my grandmother, Mamie Lee Ross Reid (1895-1991); my aunt, Ruth Reid McCall (1925-1994), my aunt, Kathleen Reid (b1928), my mother-in-law, Cassie Pittman Pruett (1910-1988), and my beloved mother, Sara Reid McMahon (b1923). Each oval is filled with memories, family stories, fragments of conversation, and random thoughts that relate to precious moments.

## PRIDE & JOY
**Deb Richardson**
*Ewing, Kentucky*
*16" x 17"*

**Materials:** *Cottons, beads, acrylic paint*
**Techniques:** *Raw-edge machine appliqué, machine quilting*

My mom was a great mother, who always made sure I knew I was loved. She was also a fabulous grandmother and used to say, *"If I'd known how fun it is to be a grandma, I would have wanted to do this first!"* My quilt is based on a snapshot of my mother, Anita Louise McNeil Keeton (1939-2001), with one of the great joys of her life—her oldest grandchild, Amber Louise Keeton. Mom has been gone nearly two years, and I still miss her every day.

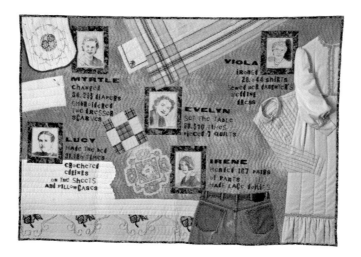

## HOUSEHOLD TEXTILES
### Kathleen Loomis
*Louisville, Kentucky*
81" x 55"

**Materials:** *Cotton, vintage and antique textiles, pre-quilted hand-dyed base fabric*
**Techniques:** *Appliqué, fabric printing using old wood and metal type, photo transfer*

I love old textiles, whether from my own family or the flea market. I feel almost mystically connected to the women who made them. Some of these textiles are family pieces; others came to me through serendipity. We all sit with our needles and contemplate our lives as we sew, finding joy, peace, and a brief respite from chores and chaos. My grandmother crocheted the edging on these pillowcases; my mother, Viola Burtzloff Arnold (b1915), made this wedding dress for my sister, Bethany. Our lives are stitched together with love.

## FROM MOTHER TO DAUGHTER
### Gisha Wogier
*Kefar Yona, Israel*
51" x 51"

**Materials:** *Fabric—recycled, hand-dyed, marbled, stamped, color discharged*
**Techniques:** *Machine piecing, hand and machine quilting*

In her youth my mother, Golda Lerch (1915-1986), had a workshop for household linens where she sewed dowries for brides. She sewed her own dowry with the extra money she earned. At the beginning of the Second World War, my young parents decided to run away from Poland to Russia to save their lives, taking some family pictures, clothes, and the dowry that my mother had prepared. In the war they sold items from the dowry for food. My father insisted they should keep some items to show to their future children. In my youth, I loved it when my mother used the linen she had made and always asked her about it. My mother was touched by my interest and promised that she would save it for my marriage. For this exhibit, it was time to take one of the four pillowcases and incorporate it into a quilt to honor my parents: my mother for sewing it and my father who didn't let her sell it. May they rest in peace.

### NURTURING LIFE
**Dot Chauncey Porter and Beth Porter Johnson**
*Tullahoma, Tennessee*
64" x 64"

**Materials:** *Cotton, some hand-dyed, Prismatic foil*
**Techniques:** *Fabrics overprinted with acrylics and pastels, appliqué*

In 1996, at the encouragement of my mother, I—a painter and non-quilter—attended the International Quilt Festival in Houston. Sharing my excitement about what I had seen, my mother Dot, also a painter and a novice quilt artist, suggested we design a quilt together.

Choosing to honor women's nurturing qualities, we created a mandala of mother figures whose hands cradle paper dolls, symbols of humanity. Not only was the experience of working together uniquely gratifying but also the subject matter resonates a deep chord within us. Like the women in our quilt, our mothers have loved us without constraints.

## ELEANOR ROPPLE
**Amy Ropple**
*Woburn, Massachusetts*
31" x 28"

---

**Materials:** *Silk, cotton, glass beads, silk flowers*
**Techniques:** *Piecing, collage, quilting, beading*

---

This portrait quilt of my mother, Eleanor Barrett Ropple (1929-2001), is based on a surprise photograph that I took one day while she talked on the telephone. She did not like having her picture taken, so this was a lucky shot of a little lady full of strong character, great humor, and much kindness. This quilt is especially meaningful to me. My artwork is often about preservation of a subject through capturing or recreating its identity in fabric. When making this portrait, I was unaware that my mother had less than a year to live. A few months before her death, she attended an exhibit where she saw her portrait on display and was both proud and honored to have been represented in this quilt.

"Mother: the most *beautiful word* on the lips of mankind."

–KAHLIL GIBRAN

## BEYOND ECCENTRIC AND PUSHING CRAZY
### Corinne Appleton
*Saskatoon, Saskatchewan, Canada*
47" x 47"

**Materials:** *Cotton, buttons, rubber stamps*
**Techniques:** *Machine piecing, hand appliqué and embellishment*

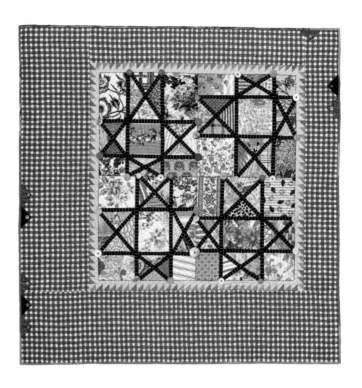

A turbulent period between my mother—E. Kathleen Down Appleton (b1935)—and myself when nothing seemed orderly, smooth, or easy to work out is represented here. The black dividers of the stars kept us from total chaos ensuring that the "crazy" bits of fabric beneath them stayed steady and allowed us to work through our differences. The large border was a note as to the amount of space we often needed from one another before we were ready to make another go of the relationship.

## TO MOM, WHO DIED WAY TOO YOUNG
### Marni Goldshlag
*Durham, North Carolina*
40" x 48"

**Materials:** *Fabric, some hand-dyed, chenille yarn*
**Techniques:** *Machine piecing, hand appliqué, knitting, writing*

My mother, Ruth Zalisch Goldshlag (1916-1973), died of lung cancer when she was not quite 57 years old and I was not quite 25. I spent many years dealing unsuccessfully with my grief. Then, in 1997, I heard a hospice counselor on the radio talking about the five things that people need to say to their loved ones before they die—*please forgive me; I forgive you; thank you; I love you; goodbye.* I never had the chance to say those things to my mother when she was alive, so I decided to say them in a quilt: a heart for the big-hearted person that she was, knitted, clean lungs to counteract the cancer which killed her, roots representing her sturdy, centered being, and roses for love. The bird flying away is my grief being given wings and permission to leave. And, for the most part, it has.

## ANGEL BLANKIE
**Amanda Onchulenko**
*Winnipeg, Manitoba, Canada*
*25" x 15"*

**Materials:** *Vellum, handmade paper, silk ribbon and thread, feathers*
**Techniques:** *Embroidery, hand piecing, machine quilting*

*Angel Blankie* was a pursuit of the soul and a gift. A few days prior to her delivery date, my cousin Saxon's wife, Lisa, went to a pre-natal doctor's appointment where she sadly discovered, at the end of her trouble-free pregnancy, that the baby had died. Days later, she had to endure natural labor to deliver a stillborn child.

A baby blanket for grieving parents needed to be a comfort yet also convey fragility, innocence, and commemoration. I imagined baby Rex as an angel. I basted a selection of handmade papers and vellums to a paper foundation to represent an assortment of fabrics. Baby Rex's newborn footprints were appliqued to the top. I used feathers for loft, iridescence for his wings, silk for his baby hair, and flecks of gold leaf to infer his treasured presence. Finally, the quilt was crowned with feathers.

## MEMORY OF MOM
**Susan Shie**
*Wooster, Ohio*
*9" x 10"*

**Materials:** *Cloth, glass beads, gemstones*
**Techniques:** *Hand embroidery, hand quilting and beading*

I started this quilt about my mother, Marie Snyder Shie (1917-2001), during my week's vigil with her, before she died. She was in a light coma, and I drew her with a pen, on the quilt's surface and started stitching it. Soon after her death, I also made 12 paintings on canvas and wrote a simple book about her life which can be read on my website, www.turtle-moon.com, in the Zodiac Gallery, in the Gallery link. My mother taught me not only how to sew precisely, in the classic way, but so many other things. She deserves to be honored all I can!

## SHE GAVE ME WINGS
**Lesley Riley**
*Bethesda, Maryland*
26" x 38"

**Materials:** *Cotton, synthetics, paper, paint, feather wings*
**Techniques:** *Bonded and painted fabric, image transfer, machine appliqué, piecing, and quilting*

My mama gave me wings. Sheltered and protected by her own softly feathered wings, she taught me how to unfold my own. I was raised to fly. Guided by her gentle nudging and encouragement, I fluttered, flapped, fell, and eventually flew from that nest we call home. My mother, June Proffit Jackson (b1925), is a beautiful woman. In this quilt, I wanted to convey the passage of time and the beauty of the rich patinas that come with age.

## IN THE WINTER OF MY YEARS I CAN STILL SEE SPRINGTIME

**Carolyn Mazloomi**
*West Chester, Ohio*
44" x 49"
From the collection of the Rocky Mountain Quilt Museum

**Materials:** *Cotton, silk, cotton yarn*
**Techniques:** *Machine and hand appliqué, machine quilting*

The moon and sun in the windows symbolize the fact that a mother's job is 24 hours a day, seven days a week. This quilt is dedicated to all the mothers who have raised their children and earned the right to *"sit back and smell the roses."* Her station is sacred. As "first educators" of their children, mothers are the most influential people on the planet. The mother is the primary source of empowerment of the individual, without which social transformation and the advancement of civilization would be impossible. I never knew my birth mother; however, I have been blessed with many mothers and grandmothers—strong women I've met over the last 20 years in the quilt community.

## 10 UP, 10 DOWN AND 10 TO GO

**Claire Anne Gabrielsen Teagan**
*Highland, Michigan*
54" x 52"

**Materials:** *Cotton*
**Techniques:** *Discharge, machine piecing and quilting*

The title of this quilt says it all. "10 Up" is the ten months, tens of pounds and tens of inches motherhood brings. "10 Down" is the tens of pounds and inches to lose and the ten months (or years!) it takes to lose them. The "10 To Go" is the ten pounds and inches left. My daughter, Elisabet Irene Teagan (b1991), who was five when I made this quilt, named it the *Laughing Quilt* because everyone laughs when they see it.

### GRACE
**Charlotte Warr Andersen**
*Salt Lake City, Utah*
48" x 58"
From a private collection

**Techniques:** *Hand appliqué, machine piecing, hand quilting*

Jim Bagley and I talked about my making a quilt for him for years. When I suggested I do a portrait of his mother, Grace, he loved the idea. I have known Grace Elizabeth Matthews Bagley (b1923) for 20 years, since getting into the business of quilting. She is one of the loveliest and most lovable of people, and I was enthusiastic about making a quilt with her beautiful face on it. I also incorporated details from her life pictorially and symbolically, as well as using traditional patchwork quilt motifs to carry out the theme.

## IT ALL STARTED WITH GRANDMA
**Pat DaRif**
*Louisville, Kentucky*
*61" x 61"*

**Materials:** *Cotton, two vintage quilt blocks*
**Techniques:** *Machine piecing, hand appliqué, hand
and machine quilting*

My grandmother, Bertha Tempel Heeke (1892-1974), introduced me to quilting, and my mother, Helen Heeke Hagan (1911-1991), taught me to sew. My grandmother and my mother opened up the world of fiber art to me. Both were creative women who primarily expressed themselves with needle and thread. My grandmother was the quilter. She was a farmer's wife who raised nine children, worked in the fields, put out a garden, and made clothing, all in the days before electricity. No matter how tired she must have been, she always had a quilt in progress. My mother, too, cherished the tiny bits of time she had to sew, after housework, children, and a part-time job. Together, these women gave me the greatest gift of my life, and I fondly remember them every time I pick up my needle and thread.

## MOTHER BETTY
### Anne Theobald
*Greenwood Village, Colorado*
*33" x 25"*

**Materials:** *Cottons, found objects, computer to cloth photos, buttons*
**Techniques:** *Free appliqué, machine appliqué and quilting*

My mother, Betty Matheny Martin (1900-1996), moved here 18 years before her death at 96 so I could take care of her. This art quilt is a memory of her—the World's Fair in 1933; the flowers from her wedding hat; her love of art, travel, and homemaking; and the white gloves for the proper lady.

## SENILE DEMENTIA
### Kate Kline
*Tulsa, Oklahoma*
*32" x 40"*

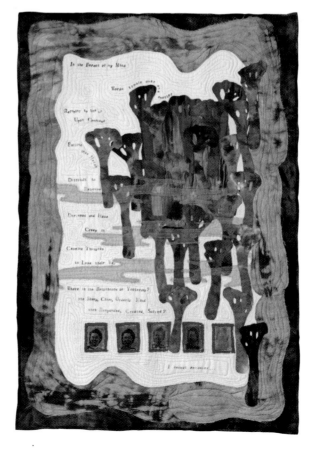

**Materials:** *Hand-dyed cotton and rayon, photo transfers, paint*
**Techniques:** *Hand and machine appliqué, sheer overlay, photo transfer, machine quilting*

This quilt is a visual interpretation of a poem that I wrote for my mother—Helen Adams Kline (1912-1992)—who suffered from senile dementia.

*In the forest of my mind,*
*words tumble over one another,*
*refusing to line up upon command,*
*falling into holes, difficult to retrieve.*
*Darkness and haze creep in,*
*causing thoughts to lose their way.*
*Where is the brightness of yesterday?*
*The sharp, clear, orderly mind that responded, created, solved?*
*I cannot remember.*

## ONE FINE DAY
**Anne Copeland**
*Lomita, California*
12" x 18"

**Materials:** *Cotton*
**Techniques:** *Machine appliqué, quilting and embroidery, hand painting*

This is my mom—Viola Agnes Lloyd (1921-2002)—the day after my baby brother, Bobby, was born on July 6, 1945. This photo of Mom, Dad, baby Bobby, and me on the bridge surrounded by the big sky symbolizes this day that was her "bridge" to the promise of the future. It was a good time, a time of wonder and of hope. This was a day when everything was right in my mom's world, hence the title, *One Fine Day.*

## MY GRAM
**Barbara A. Stewart**
*Miami, Florida*
30" x 30"

**Materials:** *Cotton*
**Techniques:** *Appliqué silhouette, hand quilting*

Mary Elizabeth Durant King (1872-1961), my little gramma, was only 4' 10" tall and there I was at 5' 8" tall and only 12 years old. Gran knew something had to be done, so she came and taught me to sew. Finally, clothes that fit. Later on, she taught me to crochet, knit, and then to quilt. I asked, "*How do you quilt?*" And she replied, "*It's just like basting, only smaller stitches.*" And so, I began to quilt.